K

W9-BXN-819

Learn to Knit

Learn to Knit

25 QUICK AND EASY KNITTING PROJECTS TO GET YOU STARTED

Fiona Goble

CICO BOOKS
LONDON NEW YORK

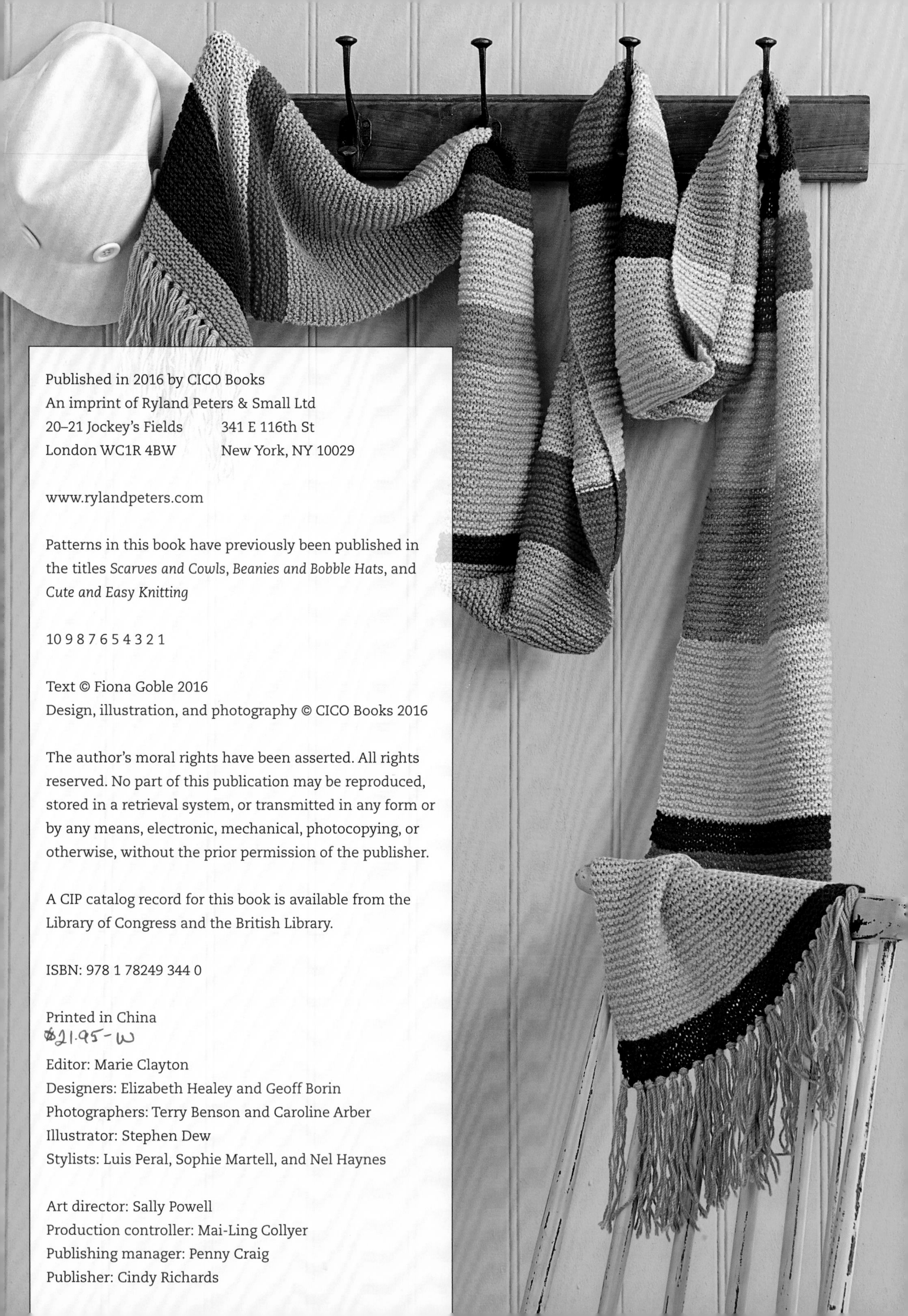

Published in 2016 by CICO Books
An imprint of Ryland Peters & Small Ltd
20–21 Jockey's Fields   341 E 116th St
London WC1R 4BW   New York, NY 10029

www.rylandpeters.com

Patterns in this book have previously been published in
the titles *Scarves and Cowls*, *Beanies and Bobble Hats*, and
Cute and Easy Knitting

10 9 8 7 6 5 4 3 2 1

Text © Fiona Goble 2016
Design, illustration, and photography © CICO Books 2016

The author's moral rights have been asserted. All rights
reserved. No part of this publication may be reproduced,
stored in a retrieval system, or transmitted in any form or
by any means, electronic, mechanical, photocopying, or
otherwise, without the prior permission of the publisher.

A CIP catalog record for this book is available from the
Library of Congress and the British Library.

ISBN: 978 1 78249 344 0

Printed in China
$21.95 – W

Editor: Marie Clayton
Designers: Elizabeth Healey and Geoff Borin
Photographers: Terry Benson and Caroline Arber
Illustrator: Stephen Dew
Stylists: Luis Peral, Sophie Martell, and Nel Haynes

Art director: Sally Powell
Production controller: Mai-Ling Collyer
Publishing manager: Penny Craig
Publisher: Cindy Richards

contents

Introduction

If you've never knitted before or haven't knitted since you were tiny and would like to knit something beautiful, this book is aimed at you. It's also for "advanced beginners" who know the basic steps, but are looking to brush up their skills and want to try some new projects.

One of the best things about knitting is how you can create a range of looks and textures from just the two basic stitches—the knit stitch and the purl stitch. And that's exactly what I've drawn on here. I firmly believe that you don't need fancy lace and cable combinations to make something impressive, just nice yarn, some needles, and a bit of time.

In the following pages, there is a section on Equipment, introducing you to the items you will need to get started. The Techniques section then shows you how to carry out all the basic skills used in the projects that follow, and commonly used terms are explained to help you make sense out of knitting patterns. Once you've practiced the techniques, you'll be ready to make some gorgeous knitted items.

All the knitting patterns included in the book have been specially selected for brand new knitters. So while you will only need novice knitting techniques, you will still be able to make some stunning items for your home and flattering accessories to wear—or of course you could give them to admiring friends and relatives! What's more, you won't have to invest huge sums in creating the first project that you can be truly proud of because almost all the patterns in this book require a few balls of yarn at most.

And once you've made a few projects, you'll probably be well on your way to becoming a knitting addict. Like the rest of us, you'll then find it hard to keep out of stores selling ball after ball of beautiful yarns, and pattern books full of exciting ideas!

I've divided the patterns inside into three categories. First there's a range of scarves and cowls to suit all tastes, from an elegant draping capelet to a scarf knitted in super-chunky stripes. Then there's a collection of beanies and bobble hats for all the family—choose from stripes, textures, and designs suitable for men, women, and children. Finally, I couldn't resist adding in a few items for the home, so feel free to deck out your rooms with some knitted bunting or get working on a stylish Scandinavian-style pillow.

Like any new skill, knitting requires a bit of practice, but the more you practice, the quicker you get and the more confident you feel. Like any craft, remember that you don't always have to do it by the book. So if you find it easier to hold your needles or yarn differently to the way we suggest, that's perfectly fine. Experiment a bit and see what feels best for you. And if you've got any comments or queries, or you would like to share your work, please contact me via my blog at fionagoble.wordpress.com.

Equipment

To get started with knitting, there are a few basic tools you will need, some of which you will probably already have.

Knitting needles

Apart from the yarn, the first thing you will need is some needles. Knitting needles are available in plastic, metal, wood, and bamboo. They come in many sizes, ranging from US size 0 (2mm) up to US size 50 (25mm), and there are even some "giant" needles larger than that. You don't need to buy every size straight away; if you are just starting to knit, buy the size recommended in the pattern, and the size above and below that, in case you need to adjust your gauge (tension)—see page 17 for advice on this. As you try out different patterns and yarns, you will gradually build up your collection of needle sizes. It is a good idea to store straight needles in a cloth roll or tube, to protect them.

Circular needles, which have pointed metal pieces at each end of a long plastic wire, are usually used for knitting in the round. They are used for the Striped College Scarf on page 82 because they can hold the large number of stitches needed, but rather than knitting in circles, for this project you knit backward and forward as you would with straight needles.

● ●

Other equipment

You will also need the following items, but if you already sew or do other crafts, you may have some of these already.

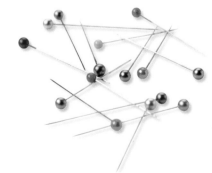

SHARP SCISSORS
You will need these for cutting yarn after binding (casting) off, and when sewing up. It is tempting to break it with your hands, but this can pull the stitches out of shape.

PINS
Rustproof, glass-headed, or T-headed quilter's pins can be used to pin knitted pieces together for sewing up. Bright-colored tops make it easy to spot the pins against the knitted fabric, so you don't leave any behind!

YARN SEWING NEEDLE

These come in various sizes, but all have large eyes for easy threading of yarn, and a blunt end which will not split the stitches when you are sewing up your work.

TAPE MEASURE

A tape measure is essential for working out gauge (tension), and for measuring your work as directed in some of the patterns.

STITCH MARKERS

These are little rings that can be slipped through stitches or on to needles to mark a particular place in your knitting.

ROW COUNTER

This is a small, tubular counter that fits on the end of your knitting needle. You turn the numbers after each row, to keep track of the total number of rows knitted.

STITCH HOLDERS

Sometimes you will need to separate out some stitches and put them on a stitch holder, while only knitting the remainder of the stitches. Stitch holders are clips with a horizontal bar that you open to slip the stitches on, and then close to keep them on the holder for later use.

POMPOM MAKER

You can make pompoms using cardboard circles cut to size (see page 27 for instructions), but these useful gadgets make creating pompoms quicker and easier.

Techniques

In this section there are instructions for all the basic knitting techniques you'll need to make the projects in this book. If you can't find the recommended yarn for a project, you can substitute a different yarn of the same type (e.g. worsted/Aran, or light worsted/DK), but you will need to check the gauge (tension) carefully. When calculating the quantity of yarn you require, don't just go by the weight of each individual ball of yarn. You need to multiply the length of yarn per ball by the number of balls needed, and compare the total with that for the replacement yarn. The length of yarn per ball in each recommended yarn is given in the patterns.

● ●

Holding needles

If you are new to knitting, you will need to find out which is the most comfortable way for you to hold your knitting needles. This applies to both a pair of knitting needles or a circular needle.

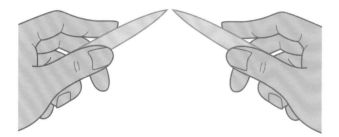

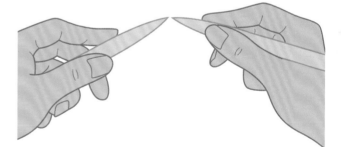

LIKE A KNIFE

Pick up one needle in each hand as if you were holding a knife and fork—with your hands over the top of each needle. As you knit, you will tuck the blunt end of the right-hand needle under your arm and let go with your hand to manipulate the yarn, returning your hand to the needle to move the stitches along.

LIKE A PEN

Hold the left-hand needle like a knife, but the right-hand needle like a pen, with your thumb and forefinger holding the needle close to the point and the shaft resting in the crook of your thumb. As you knit, do not let go of the needle but simply slide your right hand forward to manipulate the yarn.

Holding yarn

The yarn you are working with needs to be tensioned and manipulated to produce an evenly knitted fabric. You can use either your right or left hand to hold and tension the yarn, depending on the way in which you are going to make the stitches (see pages 13 and 14). Depending on your natural gauge (tension), (see page 17), you will need to wind the yarn more or less tightly around your fingers. Try the methods shown here to find out which suits you best.

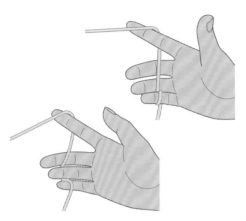

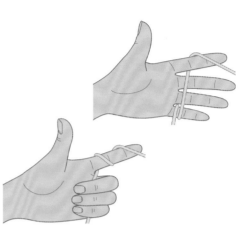

YARN IN RIGHT HAND

To knit and purl in the US/UK style (see page 13), hold the yarn in your right hand.

To hold the yarn tightly (top), wind it right around your little finger, under your ring and middle fingers, then pass it over your index finger; this finger will manipulate the yarn.

For a looser hold (bottom), catch the yarn between your little and ring fingers, pass it under your middle finger, then over your index finger.

YARN IN LEFT HAND

To knit and purl in the continental style (see page 14), hold the yarn in your left hand.

To hold the yarn tightly (top), wind it right around your little finger, under your ring and middle fingers, then pass it over your index finger; this finger will manipulate the yarn.

For a looser hold (bottom), fold your little, ring, and middle fingers over the yarn, and wind it twice around your index finger.

• •

Making a slip knot

You will need to make a slip knot to start knitting; this knot counts as the first cast-on stitch.

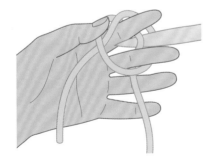

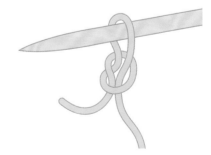

With the ball of yarn to the right, lay the end of the yarn on the palm of your left hand. With your right hand, wind the yarn twice round your index and middle fingers to make a loop. Make a second loop behind the first one. Slip a knitting needle in front of the first loop to pick up the second loop, as shown.

2 Slip the yarn off your fingers leaving the loop on the needle. Gently pull on both yarn ends to tighten the knot a little, then pull on the yarn leading to the ball of yarn to fully tighten the knot on the needle.

Casting on (cable method)

There are a few different methods of casting on, but the one used for the projects in this book is the cable method, which uses two needles.

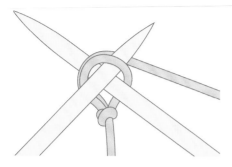

1 Make a slip knot as shown on page 11. Put the needle with the slip knot into your left hand. Insert the point of your other needle into the front of the slip knot and under the left needle. Wind the yarn from the ball of yarn around the tip of the right needle.

2 Using the tip of your needle, draw the yarn through the slip knot to form a loop. This loop is your new stitch. Slip the loop from the right needle on to the left needle.

3 To make the next stitch, insert the tip of your right needle between the two stitches. Wind the yarn over the right needle, from left to right, then draw the yarn through to form a loop. Transfer this loop to your left needle. Repeat until you have cast on the right number of stitches for your project.

• •

Thumb cast on

This method creates a cast-on row with a bit of stretch in it. Because you are working with the tail end (the cut end) of the yarn as well as the ball end, you need to estimate the length of yarn needed to cast on all the stitches required: allowing ¾in (2cm) per stitch is a safe amount.

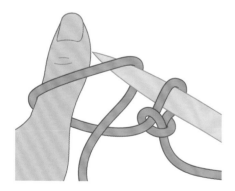

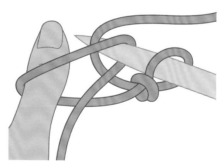

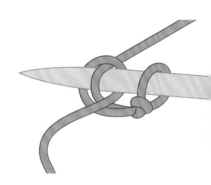

1 Measure out the required length of yarn and make a slip knot (see page 11) at that point. Hold the knitting needle in your right hand. *From front to back, wrap the tail end of the yarn around your left thumb.

2 Using your right hand, slip the point of the knitting needle under the yarn wrapped around your thumb, as shown. Wrap the ball end of the yarn around the point of the needle.

3 Pull the needle, and the yarn around it, through the loop around your thumb. Slip your left thumb out of the loop. Pull gently on the tail end of the yarn to tighten the stitch. Repeat from * until you have cast on the required number of stitches.

Knit stitch

There are only two stitches to master in knitting, and the knit stitch is the first one to learn. This is the method for making a stitch if you are knitting using the US/UK techniques, but you can also try the method known as Continental knitting (see page 14).

1 Hold the needle with the cast-on stitches in your left hand and the empty needle in your right hand. * From left to right, put the point of the right-hand needle into the front of the first stitch. Wrap the yarn round the point of the right-hand needle, again from left to right.

2 With the tip of the right-hand needle, pull the wrapped yarn through the stitch to form a loop. This loop is the new stitch.

3 Slip the original stitch off the left-hand needle by gently pulling the right-hand needle to the right. Repeat from * until you have knitted all the stitches on the left-hand needle. Swap the needles in your hands and you are ready to work the next row.

Purl stitch

This is the other stitch you need to learn, Again, this is the US/UK method, but you can try the Continental method (see page 14).

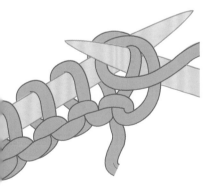  

1 Hold the needle with the cast-on stitches in your left hand and the empty needle in your right hand. * From right to left, put the point of the right-hand needle into the front of the first stitch. Wrap the yarn round the point of the right-hand needle, again from right to left.

2 With the tip of the right-hand needle, pull the wrapped yarn through the stitch to form a loop. This loop is the new stitch.

3 Slip the original stitch off the left-hand needle by gently pulling the right-hand needle to the right. Repeat from * until you have purled all the stitches on the left-hand needle. Swap the needles in your hands and you are ready to work the next row.

Knit stitch Continental method

This is how to form a knit stitch if you are holding the yarn in your left hand and so working in the Continental style. If you are left-handed, you may find this method easier than the US/UK technique (see page 13).

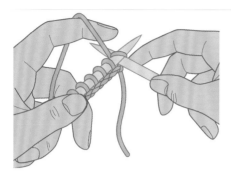
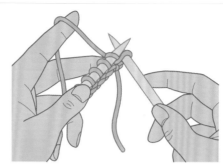
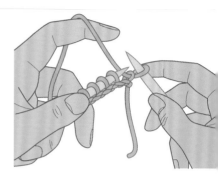

1 Hold the needle with the cast-on stitches in your left hand and the empty needle in your right hand. * From left to right, put the point of the right-hand needle into the front of the first stitch. Holding the working yarn fairly taut with your left hand at the back of the work, move the tip of the right-hand needle under the working yarn.

2 With the tip of the right-hand needle, bring the wrapped yarn through the stitch to form a loop. This loop is the new stitch.

3 Slip the original stitch off the left-hand needle by gently pulling the right-hand needle to the right. Repeat from * until you have knitted all the stitches on the left-hand needle. Swap the needles in your hands and you are ready to work th next row.

Purl stitch Continental method

Here is how a purl stitch is made when you are knitting using the Continental technique.

1 Hold the needle with the cast-on stitches in your left hand and the empty needle in your right hand. * From right to left, put the point of the right-hand needle into the front of the first stitch. Holding the working yarn fairly taut with your left hand at the back of the work, move the tip of the right-hand needle under the working yarn, then push your left index finger downward, as shown, to hold the yarn around the needle.

2 With the tip of the right-hand needle, pull the wrapped yarn through the stitch to form a loop. This loop is the new stitch.

3 Slip the original stitch off the left-hand needle by gently pulling the right-hand needle to the right. Repeat from * until you have purled all the stitches on the left-hand needle. Swap the needles in your hands and you are ready to work the next row.

inding (casting) off

When you have finished a piece of knitting, you need to bind (cast) off your stitches to stop the work nraveling. You can do this on a knit or a purl row (the pattern will tell you): it's shown here on a knit row, ut the principle is the same for a purl row, though all the stitches are purled rather than knitted.

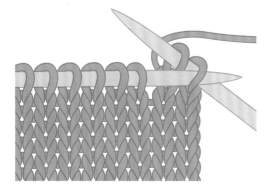

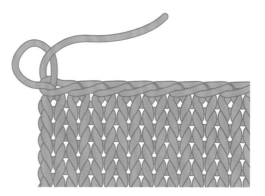

Knit the first two stitches in the usual way. * With the point of ne left-hand needle, pick up the first stitch you knitted and lift it ver the second stitch. Knit another stitch so that there are once gain two stitches on the right-hand needle. Repeat from * until here is just one stitch remaining on the right-hand needle.

2 Break the yarn, leaving a tail of yarn long enough to weave in (see page 23). Pull the tail all the way through the last stitch. Slip the stitch off the needle and pull it tight.

Basic knitted fabrics

All knitted fabrics are based on combinations of knit and purl stitches. Some of the more complex fabrics also need stitches swapped or wrapped, but they still use the basic stitches. The fabrics shown here are all very easy to knit.

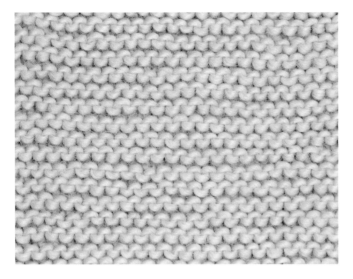

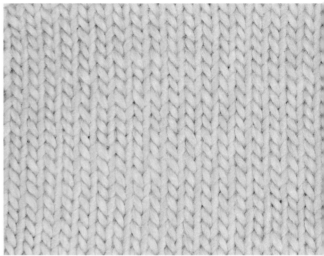

GARTER STITCH

This is the simplest of all knitted fabrics. You only need to learn knit stitch (see page 13), as every row is worked using just that stitch.

STOCKINETTE (STOCKING) STITCH

This is the most commonly used knitted fabric. To make it you work alternate rows in knit stitch and purl stitch. The "wrong" side is in fact a fabric in its own right and is called reverse stockinette (stocking) stitch.

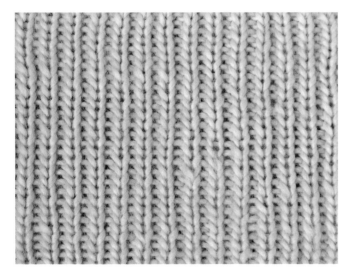

SINGLE RIB

The most commonly used type of rib stitch. This is made by working alternate knit and purl stitches. On the next row you purl the stitches that were knitted and vice versa to create the columns that make this very stretchy fabric.

DOUBLE RIB

This is made using the same principle as single rib, but you work two knit stitches followed by two purl stitches across each row.

Gauge (tension)

Gauge (called tension in the UK), is the word used to describe how tight or loose a piece of knitting is. This matters, because if your knitting is looser than that in the sample, then your project will be larger; and smaller if your knitting is tighter.

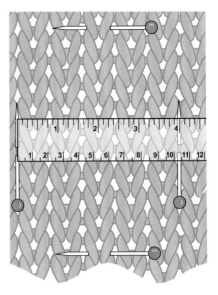

A gauge (tension) is given with each pattern to help you make your project the same size as the sample. The gauge is given as the number of stitches and rows you need to work to produce a 4-in (10-cm) square of knitting.

Using the recommended yarn and needles, cast on 8 stitches more than the gauge (tension) instruction asks for—so if you need to have 10 stitches to 4in (10cm), cast on 18 stitches. Working in the pattern as instructed, work 8 rows more than are needed. Bind (cast) off loosely.

Lay the swatch flat without stretching it. Lay a ruler across the stitches as shown,

with the 2in (5cm) mark centered on the knitting, then put a pin in the knitting at the start of the ruler and at the 4in (10cm) mark: the pins should be well away from the edges of the swatch. Count the number of stitches between the pins. Repeat the process across the rows to count the number of rows to 4in (10cm).

If the number of stitches and rows you've counted is the same as the number asked for in the instructions, you have the correct gauge (tension). If you do not have the same number, then you will need to change your gauge (tension).

To change gauge (tension) you need to

change the size of your knitting needles. A good rule of thumb to follow is that one difference in needle size will create a difference of one stitch in the gauge (tension). You will need to use larger needles to achieve fewer stitches and smaller ones to achieve more stitches.

Blocking

If, once you have finished the piece of knitting, it doesn't look as smooth and even as you hoped it would, then blocking it can help. You can also use this process to straighten or to re-shape pieces a little if need be. The precise method of blocking you use depends on the fiber the yarn is spun from: the ball band will give you advice on that.

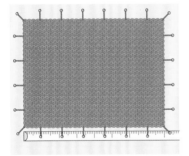

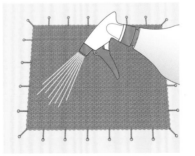

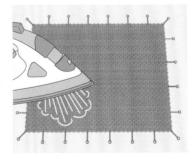

1 Lay the piece of knitting flat on an ironing board and ease it in to shape. Don't pull hard and keep the knitting flat. Starting at the corners (if there are any), pin the edges of the piece to the ironing board, pushing the pins in far enough to hold the knitting firmly. Use a ruler or tape measure to check that the pinned pieces are the right size.

2 If the fiber or texture of your yarn does not respond well to heat, then use a spray bottle of cold water to completely dampen the knitting, but do not make it soaking wet. Leave the knitting to dry naturally, then unpin it.

3 If you can use heat, then set the iron to the temperature the yarn ball band recommends. Hold the iron 1in (2.5cm) above the surface of the knitting and steam it for a couple of minutes. Move the iron so that the whole surface gets steamed, but don't actually touch the knitting with the iron as this can spoil the texture and drape of the fabric and may leave shiny patches. Leave the knitting to dry naturally, then unpin it.

Increasing

This means creating extra stitches to shape your knitting. There are two main methods used in this book, both of which have variations depending on which row you are working on, and which direction the increased stitches need to slope in to create an effect.

INCREASE ON A KNIT ROW

This is usually abbreviated as "inc" in a knitting pattern. There will be a visible bar of yarn across the base of the extra stitch.

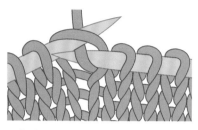

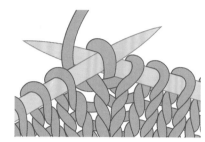

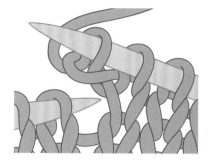

1 Knit the next stitch on the left-hand needle in the usual way (see page 13), but do not slip the original stitch off the left-hand needle.

2 Move the right-hand needle behind the left-hand needle and put it into the same stitch again, but through the back of the stitch this time. Knit the stitch through the back loop (see page 13).

3 Slip the original stitch off the left-hand needle. You have increased by one stitch.

INCREASE ON A PURL ROW

This is also usually abbreviated as "inc" when working a purl row, or "inc pwise."

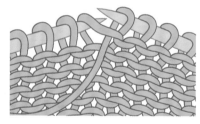

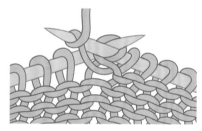

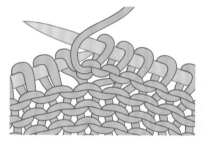

1 Purl the next stitch on the left-hand needle in the usual way (see page 13), but do not slip the original stitch off the left-hand needle.

2 Twist the right-hand needle backward to make it easier to put it into the same stitch again, but through the back of the stitch this time. Purl the stitch through the back loop (see page 13).

3 Slip the original stitch off the left-hand needle. You have increased by one stitch.

MAKE ONE LEFT ON A KNIT ROW

This method is usually abbreviated as "m1" or "m1l": if a pattern just says 'm1', this is the increase it refers to. It creates an extra stitch almost invisibly.

1 From the front, slip the tip of the left-hand needle under the horizontal strand of yarn running between the last stitch on the right-hand needle and the first stitch on the left-hand needle.

2 Put the right-hand needle knitwise into the back of the loop formed by the picked up strand and knit the loop in the same way you would knit a stitch (see page 13), but through the back loop (see page 13). You have increased by one stitch.

MAKE ONE RIGHT ON A KNIT ROW

This increase will usually be abbreviated as "m1r" in a pattern. It slopes in the opposite direction to the "make one left" increase.

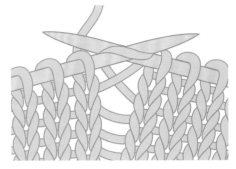

From the back, slip the tip of the left-hand needle under the horizontal strand of yarn running between the last stitch on the right-hand needle and the first stitch on the left-hand needle. Put the right-hand needle knitwise into the front of the loop formed by the picked-up strand, and knit it in the same way you would knit a stitch (see page 13). You have increased by one stitch.

MAKE ONE LEFT ON A PURL ROW

You can also use make one increases on a purl row, and this version is usually abbreviated as "m1lp" or "m1p" in a knitting pattern.

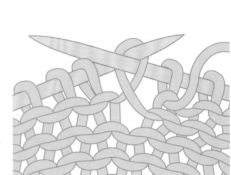

From the front, slip the tip of the left-hand needle under the horizontal strand of yarn running between the last stitch on the right-hand needle and the first stitch on the left-hand needle. Put the right-hand needle purlwise into the back of the loop formed by the picked-up strand and purl the loop in the same way you would purl a stitch (see page 13), but through the back loop (see page 13). You have increased by one stitch.

• •

Slipping stitches

Slipping stitches means simply passing them from one needle to the other without knitting or purling them. They can be slipped knitwise or purlwise, but unless stated otherwise in a pattern, slip them purlwise. Stitches are slipped for some shaping techniques (see page 18, and above), and to create some stitch patterns.

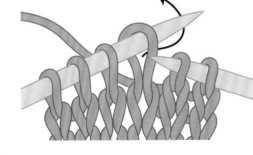

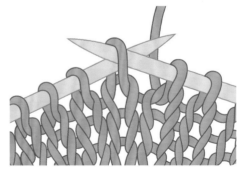

KNITWISE
From left to right, put the right-hand needle into the next stitch on the left-hand needle and slip it over onto the right-hand needle without knitting it.

PURLWISE
You can slip a stitch purlwise on a purl row or a knit row. From right to left, put the right-hand needle into the next stitch on the left-hand needle and slip it over onto the right-hand needle without purling it.

Decreasing

This means taking away stitches to shape your knitting. The technique used will depend on how many stitches need to be eliminated, and as with increasing (see pages 18–19), the methods make the stitches slope in different directions.

KNIT TWO TOGETHER

This is the simplest way of decreasing and is abbreviated to "k2tog" in a pattern.

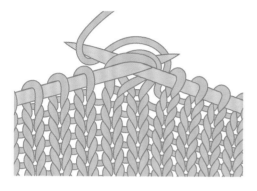

Put the right-hand needle knitwise through the next two stitches on the left-hand needle instead of through just one stitch, and then knit them in the usual way (see page 13) as if they were a single stitch. You have decreased by one stitch.

To knit three stitches together—abbreviated to "k3tog"—simply put the needle through three instead of two stitches and knit all three together.

PURL TWO TOGETHER

This is the purl row equivalent of the decrease above, and is abbreviated to "p2tog."

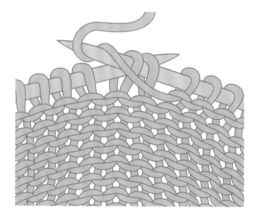

Put the right-hand needle purlwise through the next two stitches on the left-hand needle instead of through just one stitch, and then purl them in the usual way (see page 13) as if they were a single stitch. You have decreased by one stitch.

SLIP, SLIP, KNIT

This decrease requires you to slip stitches (see page 19) to twist them before knitting them together. It is abbreviated to "ssk" in a knitting pattern.

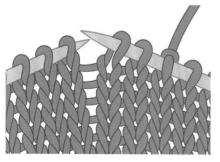

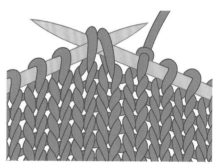

1 Slip one stitch knitwise onto the right-hand needle, and then do the same with the next stitch so two stitches have been slipped.

2 Put the left-hand needle from left to right through the front loops of both the slipped stitches and knit them in the usual way (see page 13). You have decreased by one stitch.

SLIP ONE, KNIT TWO TOGETHER, PASS THE SLIPPED STITCH OVER

Reduce the number of stitches by two using this decrease. The abbreviation for this varies; "sk2po" is used in this book, but "sk2togpo" and "sl1, k2tog, psso" are both commonly used as well.

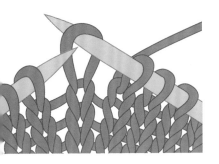

1 Slip the first stitch knitwise from the left-hand to the right-hand needle (see page 19).

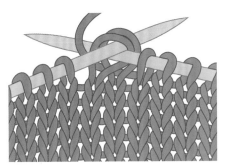

2 Knit the next two stitches on the left-hand needle together (see page 13).

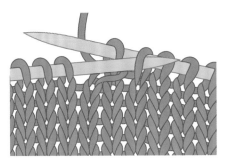

3 Finally, lift the slipped stitch over the knitted stitch and drop it off the needle. You have decreased by two stitches.

SLIP TWO, KNIT ONE, PASS THE SLIPPED STITCHES OVER (SL2, K1, PSSO)

This method places the center stitch of the three that are worked together on top and therefore maintains a straight look to the work.

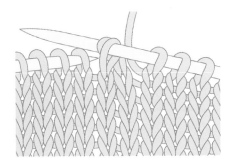

1 Insert the right-hand needle into the next two stitches on the left-hand needle, as if you were about to k2tog. Instead, slip them onto the right-hand needle and do not knit them.

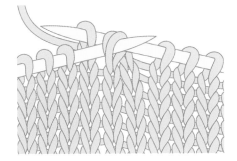

2 Knit the next stitch as normal, then lift the two slipped stitches over the knitted stitch and off the right-hand needle.

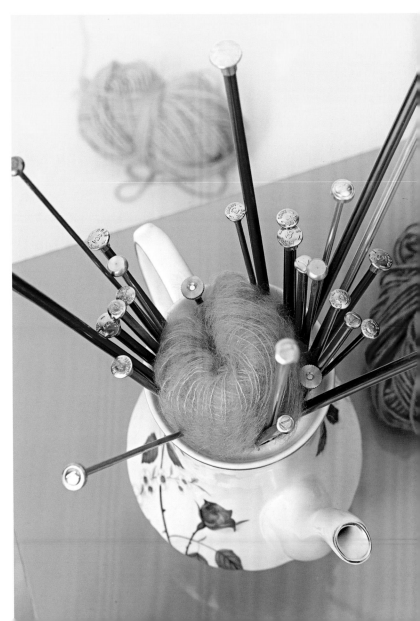

Stranding

Often referred to as "Fair Isle," this is the method of color knitting for patterns that go over a whole row. If you haven't tried it before, then it's a good idea to try it out on swatches before starting a project, as getting the gauge (tension) of the yarns right can take a bit of practice. These instructions are for the simplest method of stranding, where you work holding one yarn at a time.

CHANGING COLOR ON A KNIT ROW

It's important to swap the yarns in the right way when changing colors to keep the fabric flat and smooth.

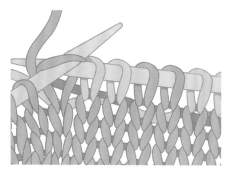

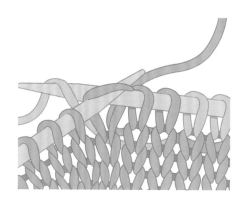

1 Knit the stitches (see page 13) in color A (brown in this example), bringing the yarn across over the strand of color B (lime in this example) to wrap around the needle.

2 At the color change, drop color A and pick up color B, bringing it across under the strand of color A to wrap around the needle. Be careful not to pull it too tight. Knit the stitches in color B. When you change back to color A, bring it across over the strand of color B.

CHANGING COLOR ON A PURL ROW

You can clearly see how the colors are swapped when working the purl rows.

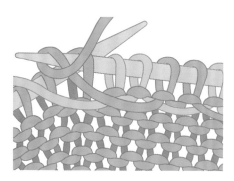

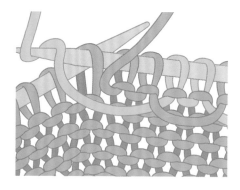

1 Purl the stitches (see page 13) in color A (brown in this example), bringing it across over the strand of color B (lime in this example) to wrap around the needle.

2 At the color change, drop color A and pick up color B, bringing it across under the strand of color A to wrap around the needle. Be careful not to pull it too tight. Purl the stitches in color B. When you change back to color A, bring it across over the strand of color B.

Weaving in yarns

If the gap between color changes is more than five stitches—or as few as three stitches on thicker yarns—you need to weave the stranded yarns together at intervals. The yarn that you're not using is twisted around the color that you're working with. Alternate between twisting clockwise and counterclockwise to prevent the yarn getting too tangled up.

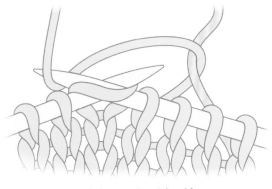

Twisting on the right side

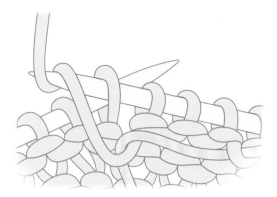

Twisting on the wrong side

Joining in a new color

You will usually bring in a new color (as directed in the pattern) at the beginning of a row.

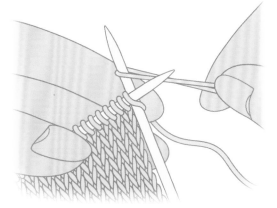

1 Break the old yarn, leaving a 4-6in (10-15cm) tail. Insert the needle into the next stitch to be knitted, then knit it in the new color as usual, leaving a 4-6in (10-15cm) tail of the new color yarn.

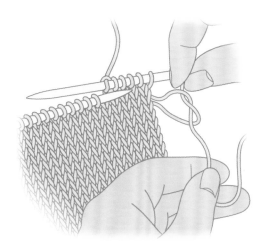

2 Knit a few more stitches in the new color, then tie the tails together with a single knot to stop the loose first stitch falling off the needle. Don't use a double knot as this will make it difficult to sew the ends in later, and the knot will eventually work itself out of the knitting.

Intarsia

This method of color knitting is used for motifs rather than for overall patterns. You need a separate bobbin or ball of yarn for each area of color. It's vital to twist the yarns in the right way to link the areas of color and avoid holes appearing in the knitting, so if this is a new technique for you, do practice on a swatch before starting a project.

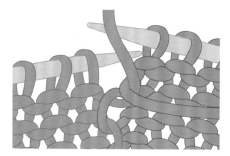 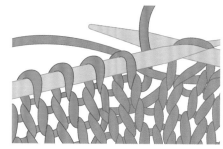 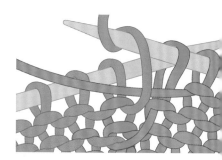

VERTICAL COLOR CHANGE

Don't rush adjusting and linking the yarns on straight vertical color changes as the stitches can become loose.

1 On a purl row (see page 13), work to the last stitch in the old color (pink in this example). Bring the new color (gray in this example) from under the old color and purl the next stitch firmly.

The same principle applies on a knit row. Work to the last stitch in the old color, then bring the new color under the old color and purl the next stitch firmly.

COLOR CHANGE ON A SLANT

Where the color change runs in a sloping line, you need to be careful that the yarns are properly linked around one another at the change.

1 On a knit row (see page 13), work to the last stitch in the old color (gray in this example). Put the left-hand needle knitwise into this stitch, then bring the new color (pink in this example) across under the old color, wrap it around the tip of the right-hand needle, and knit the stitch in the new color.

2 On a purl row (see page 13), work to the last stitch in the new color (pink in this example). Put the left-hand needle purlwise into the next stitch on the left-hand needle, then bring the old color (gray in this example) up under the new color and purl the stitch in the old color.

Carrying yarn up the side of the work

When you knit stripe patterns you do not need to join in a new color for every stripe. Instead, carry the color not in use up the side of the work until you need it again.

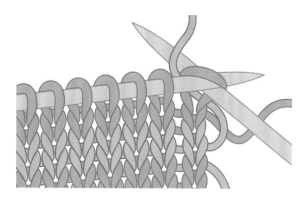 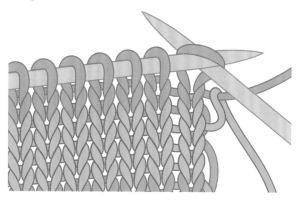

1 If the stripes change every two rows, then just bring the yarn not in use up and knit with it as needed.

2 If the stripes are wider, then you need to catch in the yarn not in use at the ends of rows to prevent long, loose strands appearing. To do this, put the right-hand needle into the first stitch of a row, lay the yarn to be carried over the working yarn, and then knit the stitch in the working yarn.

ewing up

ifferent sewing stitches work best on different knitted fabrics and types
f seams. The patterns will tell you which stitch to use on a project.

EWING IN ENDS

se a large-eyed yarn sewing needle (or a tapestry needle), which has a blunt tip, to
eave the yarn end in and out of a few stitches. (The end is shown here in a contrast
olor for clarity.) Alternatively, if there is a seam to sew then you can leave a very long
nd and sew the seam with it.

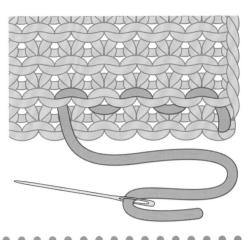

FLAT STITCH

Unlike mattress stitch (below), this creates a seam that is completely flat.

Lay the two edges to be joined side by side with the right sides facing you. Using a
yarn sewing needle, pick up the very outermost strand of knitting from one side and
then the other, working your way along the seam and pulling the yarn up firmly every
few stitches.

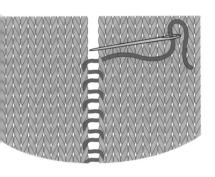

MATTRESS STITCHING ROW-END EDGES

he seam is worked from the right side and will be almost invisible.

Right sides up, lay the two edges to be joined side by side. Thread a yarn sewing needle
ith a long length of yarn. From the back bring the needle up between the first and
econd stitches of the left-hand piece, immediately above the cast-on edge. Take it across
o the right-hand piece, and from the back bring it through between the first and second
titches of that piece, immediately above the cast-on edge. Take it back to the left-hand
iece and, again from the back, bring it through one row above where it first came
hrough, between the first and second stitches. Pull the yarn through and this figure-of-
ight will hold the cast-on edges level.

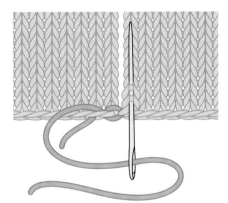

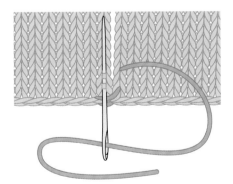

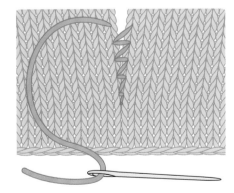

*Take the needle across to the right-hand piece and, from the
ront, take it under the bars of yarn between the first and second
titches on the next two rows up. Take the needle across to the
eft-hand piece and, from the front, take it under the bars of yarn
etween the first and second stitches on the next two rows up.

3 Repeat from * to sew up the seam. When you have sewn about
1in (2.5cm), gently and evenly pull the stitches tight to close the
seam, and then continue.

MATTRESS STITCHING CAST-ON OR BOUND- (CAST-) OFF EDGES

You can either gently pull the sewn stitches taut but have them visible, as shown, or you can pull them completely tight so that they disappear.

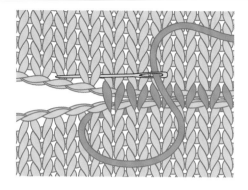

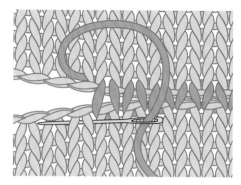

1 Right sides up, lay the two edges to be joined side by side. Thread a yarn sewing needle with a long length of yarn. Secure the yarn on the back of the lower knitted piece, then bring the needle up through the middle of the first whole stitch in that piece. Take the needle under both loops of the first whole stitch on the upper piece, so that it comes to the front between the first and second stitches.

2 *Go back into the lower piece and take the needle through to the back where it first came out, and then bring it back to the front in the middle of the next stitch along. Pull the yarn through. Take the needle under both loops of the next whole stitch on the upper piece. Repeat from * to sew the seam.

Crochet chain stitch

While the projects in this book are all knitted, some require a crochet chain.

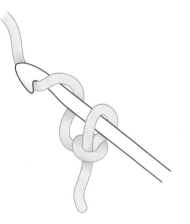

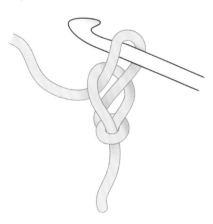

1 Make a slip knot on the crochet hook in the same way as for knitting (see page 11). Holding the resulting slip stitch on the hook, wind the yarn round the hook from the back to the front, then catch the yarn in the crochet-hook tip.

2 Pull the yarn through the slip stitch on the crochet hook to make the second link in the chain. Continue in this way until the chain is the length that you need.

Making pompoms

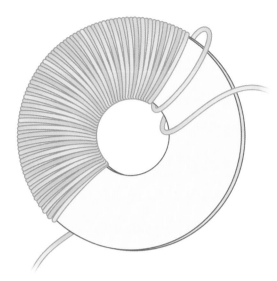

Using either a pair of card rings cut to the size pompom you would like to create, or a pompom maker in the desired size, cut a length of yarn and wind it around the rings until the rings are completely full. You can use more than one color of yarn for a multicolored pompom by using shorter lengths of each color and switching between them.

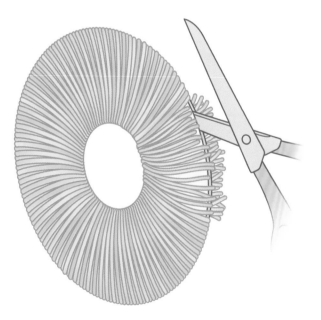

Cut through the loops around the outer edge of the rings and ease them slightly apart. Thread a length of yarn between the layers and tie tightly, leaving a long end. Remove the card rings and fluff up the pompom. Use the long tail to stitch it in place very securely. Trim off the yarn tail and any odd long ends.

CHAPTER 1

Scarves AND Cowls

Pompom scarf

With its giant fluffy pompoms, this scarf is a great way to make a statement—without much effort. You can make the pompoms with a special pompom maker (but beware; they are addictive!) or you can create your own pompom maker with nothing more sophisticated than a sheet of card. Knitted in 100 percent wool, this generously sized scarf is guaranteed to keep you mega-cozy.

• •

Skills needed:

● **Cast on** ● **Bind (cast) off** ● **Knit** ● **Purl** ● **Making pompoms**

YARN
Rowan Cocoon (80% merino wool, 20% mohair) bulky (chunky) yarn:
  2 x 3½oz (100g) balls (126yd/115m) in shade 825 Clay (A)
  1 x 3½oz (100g) ball (126yd/115m) in shade 813 Seascape (B)

NEEDLES AND EQUIPMENT
US size 10½ (7mm) knitting needles
Yarn sewing needle
Pompom maker to make 4½in (11.5cm) pompoms (see page 27), or four cardboard circles each measuring 4½in (11.5cm) in diameter with a 2¼in (5.5cm) diameter hole in the center

GAUGE (TENSION)
14 sts and 16 rows in stockinette (stocking) stitch to a 4-in (10-cm) square on US size 10½ (7mm) needles.

MEASUREMENTS
The finished scarf is 62in (158cm) long and 11½in (29cm) wide.

ABBREVIATIONS
k = knit
p = purl
rep = repeat
st(s) = stitch(es)

For the scarf
Cast on 34 sts in A.
Row 1: K.
Row 2: P.
Row 3: K.
Row 4: K.
Rep these 4 rows 47 times more.
Row 193: K.
Row 194: P.
Row 195: K.
Bind (cast) off.

Making up and finishing
Gather the short ends of the scarf using the yarn tails left from casting on and binding (casting) off.

Using the pompom maker or cardboard circles (see page 27), make two large pompoms in B, using half the ball for each pompom. Trim the pompoms and use the tails of yarn to sew one to each scarf end.

Weave in all loose ends.

chunky ribbed cowl

Skills needed:

- Cast on
- Bind (cast) off
- Knit
- Purl
- Rib
- Follow pattern repeats

Pull it up a bit... pull it down a bit... fold it over... this has go to be one of the most adaptable pieces of neckwear ever. What's more, it involves no fancy shaping and no fancy stitches. In fact, once you've got started, you could practicall knit it in your sleep. And did I mention that it's suitable for teens, men, and women. What's not to like?

YARN
Debbie Bliss Rialto Chunky (100% merino wool) bulky (chunky) yarn:
  3 x 1¾oz (50g) balls (66yd/60m) in
  shade 19 Aqua

NEEDLES AND EQUIPMENT
US size 10½ (6.5mm) knitting needles
Yarn sewing needle

GAUGE (TENSION)
15 sts and 21 rows in stockinette (stocking) stitch to a 4-in (10-cm) square on US size 10½ (6.5mm) needles.

MEASUREMENTS
The cowl is 9in (23cm) wide (unstretched) and 12in (30cm) deep.

ABBREVIATIONS
k = knit
p = purl
rep = repeat
st(s) = stitch(es)
[ ] = denotes a sequence of stitches to be repeated the number of times given after the brackets

For the cowl
Cast on 102 sts.
Row 1: [K3, p3] to end.
Row 2: [P3, k3] to end.
These 2 rows form the rib pattern.
Rep rows 1–2, 22 times more.
Bind (cast) off in the rib pattern.

Making up and finishing
Sew the row-end edges of the knitting together using mattress stitch (see page 25). Weave in all loose ends.

Long striped scarf

A certain TV character has been adorning his retro wardrobe with something a little like this for many a year—and now it's your turn to get in on the act. It's long—so it's not the quickest scarf to knit. But as it's knitted entirely in garter stitch, it's very simple. And so long as you're the patient sort, and you're happy to while away quite a few hours knitting, this could be the perfect project to get your teeth into. I've knitted it in seven shades of the same type of yarn—but if you've got a stash of light worsted (DK) yarns that you're dying to get rid of, just work it in stripes of your choice. For a scarf of the length shown here, you will need a total of approximately 1250yd/1143m of yarn.

Skills needed:

- **Cast on**
- **Bind (cast) off**
- **Knit**
- **Join in new color**
- **Making tassels**

YARN

Sirdar Country Style DK (40% nylon, 30% wool, 30% acrylic) light worsted (DK) yarn:

1 x 1¾oz (50g) ball (170yd/155m) in shade 530 Chocolate (A)
2 x 1¾oz (50g) balls (170yd/155m) in shade 399 Honey (B)
1 x 1¾oz (50g) ball (170yd/155m) in shade 394 Amber (C)
1 x 1¾oz (50g) ball (170yd/155m) in shade 599 Apples (D)
1 x 1¾oz (50g) ball (170yd/155m) in shade 396 Rustic Red (E)
1 x 1¾oz (50g) ball (170yd/155m) in shade 389 Smokey Stone (F)
2 x 1¾oz (50g) balls (170yd/155m) in shade 477 Mink (G)

NEEDLES AND EQUIPMENT

US size 6 (4mm) knitting needles
Yarn sewing needle
Medium size crochet hook for attaching the tassels (optional)

GAUGE (TENSION)

22 sts and 28 rows in stockinette (stocking) stitch to a 4-in (10-cm) square on US size 6 (4mm) needles.

MEASUREMENTS

The finished scarf is 3½yd (3.2m) long (excluding tassels) and 12in (30cm) wide.

ABBREVIATIONS

k = knit
st(s) = stitch(es)

For the scarf

Cast on 50 sts in A.
K 10 rows.
Break A and join in B.
K 50 rows.
Break B and join in C.
K 14 rows.
Break C and join in D.
K 10 rows.
Break D and join in E.
K 20 rows.
Break E and join in A.
K 8 rows.
Break A and join in F.
K 44 rows.
Break F and join in G.
K 26 rows.
Break G and join in D.
K 8 rows.
Break D and join in B.
K 34 rows.
Break B and join in E.
K 16 rows.
Break E and join in C.
K 8 rows.
Break C and join in A.
K 12 rows.
Break A and join in G.
K 46 rows.
Break G and join in D.
K 10 rows.
Break D and join in F.
K 18 rows.
Break F and join in E.
K 10 rows.
Break E and join in B.
K 46 rows.
Break B and join in A.
K 10 rows.

Break A and join in G.
K 22 rows.
Break G and join in F.
K 14 rows.
Break F and join in D.
K 8 rows.
Break D and join in E.
K 20 rows.
Break E and join in A.
K 8 rows.
Break A and join in C.
K 40 rows.
Break C and join in B.
K 12 rows.
Break B and join in F.
K 10 rows.
Break F and join in E.
K 24 rows.
Break E and join in D.
K 16 rows.
Break D and join in G.
K 36 rows.
Break G and join in A.
K 8 rows.
Break A and join in B.
K 42 rows.
Break B and join in C.
K 12 rows.
Break C and join in F.
K 22 rows.
Break F and join in E.
K 8 rows.
Break E and join in A.
K 16 rows.
Break A and join in B.
K 8 rows.
Break B and join in D.
K 20 rows.
Break D and join in G.
K 50 rows.

Break G and join in E.
K 12 rows.
Break E and join in F.
K 14 rows.
Break F and join in D.
K 10 rows.
Break D and join in A.
K 26 rows.
Break A and join in C.
K 12 rows.
Bind (cast) off.

Making up and finishing

For the tassels, cut 39 x 11-in (28-cm) lengths of yarns C and D and cut 36 x 11-in (28-cm) lengths of B and G. For each tassel, hold three strands of yarn together, fold the bundle in half, push the folded end through the knitting (using the crochet hook if you wish), then loop the cut ends through the folded end. In this way, attach 25 tassels along the cast-on edge, alternating yarns C and G and beginning and ending with a tassel in C: you will need to attach a tassel to approximately every other cast-on stitch. In a similar way, arrange 25 tassels along the bound- (cast-) off edge, alternating yarns D and B, beginning and ending with a tassel in D.

Weave in all loose ends.

Simple capelet

Skills needed:

- Cast on
- Bind (cast) off
- Knit
- Purl
- Follow pattern repeats
- Sewing on button

It may surprise you to discover that this stylish capelet is a simple knitted rectangle. What's more, to create it you need know nothing more than how to cast on and bind (cast) off, and how to work the knit and purl stitches. So if you want something that's impressive as well as easy, this is definitely the project for you.

YARN

Rowan Baby Merino Silk DK (66% wool, 34% silk) light worsted (DK) yarn:
  2 x 1¾oz (50g) balls (148yd/135m) in shade 686 Cantaloupe

NEEDLES AND EQUIPMENT

US size 6 (4mm) knitting needles
Yarn sewing needle

OTHER MATERIALS

1⅜in (35mm) button in dark red

GAUGE (TENSION)

22 sts and 30 rows in stockinette (stocking) stitch to a 4-in (10cm) square on US size 6 (4mm) needles.

MEASUREMENTS

The finished cape measures 34¼in (87cm) along lower edge and is 8in (20cm) deep.

ABBREVIATIONS

k = knit
p = purl
rep = repeat
st(s) = stitch(es)
[ ] = denotes a sequence of stitches to be repeated the number of times given after the brackets

For the capelet

Cast on 48 sts.
K 2 rows.
Row 3: K4, [k1, p2] to last 5 sts, k5.
Row 4: K4, [p1, k2] to last 5 sts, p1, k4.
Row 5: K.
Row 6: K4, p to last 4 sts, k4.
Rep rows 3–6, 56 times more.
Row 231: K4, [k1, p2] to last 5 sts, k5.
Row 232: K4, [p1, k2] to last 5 sts, p1, k4.
K 2 rows.
Bind (cast) off.

Making up and finishing

Fold down 2¼in (7cm) at the top corners of both ends of the capelet and overlap the right over the left side.

Sew on the button, using the picture as a guide, taking in all the front layers so the two ends are held in place.

Fold down the top edge of the capelet to form the collar.

Weave in all loose ends.

Long scarf with pockets

This scarf is a must-have personal insulation system for those days when it's almost too cold to poke a toe outside. It's generously proportioned and there are pockets at each end to keep your hands snug. I've selected two complementary shades, but you could just as easily knit the scarf in one color—or even three or more—if you want something utterly unique. And the stitch is simple enough to work when you want to do something a little more challenging than just watching TV.

Skills needed:
- **Cast on**
- **Bind (cast) off**
- **Knit**
- **Purl**
- **Follow pattern repeats**
- **Join in a new color**

YARN
Lion Brand Wool-Ease (80% acrylic, 20% wool) worsted (Aran) yarn:
- 2 x 3oz (85g) balls (197yd/180m) in shade 191 Violet (A)
- 2 x 3oz (85g) balls (197yd/180m) in shade 123 Seaspray (B)

NEEDLES AND EQUIPMENT
US size 9 (5.5mm) knitting needles
Yarn sewing needle

OTHER MATERIALS
2 x 1½in (4cm) natural wooden buttons

GAUGE (TENSION)
16 sts and 22 rows in stockinette (stocking) stitch to a 4-in (10-cm) square on US size 9 (5.5mm) needles.

MEASUREMENTS
The finished scarf is 82½in (210cm) long and 9½in (24cm) wide.

ABBREVIATIONS
k = knit
p = purl
rep = repeat
st(s) = stitch(es)
[ ] = denotes a sequence of stitches to be repeated the number of times given after the brackets

For the scarf
Cast on 47 sts in A.
Row 1: K3, [p1, k3] to end.
Row 2: K1, [p1, k3] to last 2 sts, p1, k1.
Rep rows 1–2, 46 times more.
Row 95: K3, [p1, k3] to end.
Break A and join in B.
Row 96: K1, [p1, k3] to last 2 sts, p1, k1.
Row 97: K3, [p1, k3] to end.
Rep rows 96–97, 179 times more (or until you have used all three balls of B, ending with a Row 97).
Break B and join in A.

Row 456: K1, [p1, k3] to last 2 sts, p1, k1.
Row 457: K3, [p1, k3] to end.
Rep rows 456–457, 46 times more.
Row 550: K1, [p1, k3] to last 2 sts, p1, k1.
Bind (cast) off.

Making up and finishing
Lay the scarf down so that the side where the color-change looks neatest is uppermost. Fold up the cast-on and bound- (cast-) off edges so that they are in line with the parts of the scarf where the colors change. Sew the sides of the pocket using matching yarn and flat stitch (see page 25).

Sew the buttons in place on the top part of the pockets using a separated strand of B.

Weave in all loose ends.

Striped college scarf

If you're after a true classic, look no further than this stripy scarf. It's knitted in a super-chunky yarn so is extremely quick to knit. Best of all, you'll need to know nothing more than the standard knit stitch to create this mega-cozy number. Knit it in the college or team colors of your choice to ward off the winter chills when you're out and about or watching the game.

Skills needed:

- **Cast on**
- **Bind (cast) off**
- **Knit**
- **Join in a new color**

YARN
Rowan Big Wool (100% wool) super bulky (super-chunky) yarn:
  2 x 3½oz (100g) balls (87yd/80m) in shade 1 White Hot (A)
  1 x 3½oz (100g) balls (87yd/80m) in shade 52 Steel Blue (B)

NEEDLES AND EQUIPMENT
US size 17 (12mm) circular knitting needle at least 32in (80cm) long
Yarn sewing needle

GAUGE (TENSION)
7.5 sts and 11.5 rows in stockinette (stocking) stitch to a 4-in (10-cm) square on US size 17 (12mm) needles.

MEASUREMENTS
The scarf is 72in (184cm) long and 6in (15.5cm) wide.

ABBREVIATIONS
cont = continue
k = knit
rep = repeat
st(s) = stitch(es)

For the scarf
Cast on 145 sts in A.
K back and forth on the circular needle, not round and round. So, K the sts, transferring them from one tip of the needle to the other tip, then when you reach the end of the row, swap the tips in your hands and work back along the row.
K 2 rows in A.
Join in B, do not break A.
K 2 rows in B.
Rep these 4 rows 4 times more.
Break B and cont in A.
K 2 rows.
Bind (cast) off.

Making up and finishing
Weave in all loose ends.

Rib scarf

This beautiful, striped scarf can be worn long and loose, or wrapped around your neck quite a few times. The chunky yarn is the ideal choice for wool-sensitive people, as it's 100% acrylic yet still warm and very soft. And if you want a bit of color without the hassle of chopping and changing yarns, the self-striping feature is sheer perfection. Knitted in a simple rib stitch, it is an ideal first or second project for newbie knitters.

Skills needed:

- **Cast on**
- **Bind (cast) off**
- **Knit**
- **Purl**

YARN

Lion Brand Unique (100% acrylic) chunky yarn:
   4 x 3½oz (100g) balls (109yd/100m) in shade 201 Garden

NEEDLES AND EQUIPMENT

US size 10½ (6.5mm) knitting needles
Yarn sewing needle

GAUGE (TENSION)

14 sts and 18 rows in stockinette (stocking) stitch to a 4-in (10-cm) square on US size 10½ (6.5mm) needles.

MEASUREMENTS

The finished scarf is 72in (184cm) long and 12in (30cm) wide.

ABBREVIATIONS

k = knit
p = purl
rep = repeat
st(s) = stitch(es)

For the scarf

Cast on 45 sts.
Row 1: [K3, p3] to end.
Row 2: [P3, k3] to end.
These 2 rows form the rib pattern.
Rep rows 1 and 2 until you have used up all your yarn, or your scarf is as long as you want it.
Bind (cast) off in the rib pattern.

Making up and finishing

Weave in all loose yarn ends.

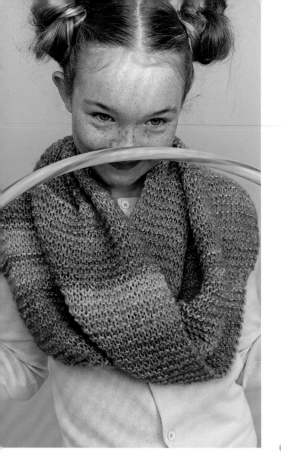

Twisted cowl

It's simple, colorful, and sweet. It's knitted entirely in garter stitch—the simplest of all stitches. And it only takes a couple of balls of yarn to complete. So now, not even the youngest and newest of knitters has any excuse not to get clicking. The yarn is variegated or "self striping"—so it creates its own stripes without you having to chop and change between balls of different colors. And remember, you can wear the finished cowl as we've shown here, or around your shoulders, so it's more like a capelet.

Skills needed:

- **Cast on**
- **Bind (cast) off**
- **Knit**
- **Joining seams**

YARN
Lion Brand Amazing (53% wool, 47% acrylic) worsted (Aran) yarn:
  2 x 1¾oz (50g) balls (147yd/135m) in shade 220 Carnival

NEEDLES AND EQUIPMENT
US size 9 (5.5mm) knitting needles
Yarn sewing needle

GAUGE (TENSION)
16 sts and 22 rows in stockinette (stocking) stitch to a 4-in (10-cm) square on US size 9 (5.5mm) needles.

MEASUREMENTS
The finished cowl measures 17in (43cm) across (unstretched) and is 15in (38cm) deep.

ABBREVIATIONS
k = knit
st(s) = stitch(es)

For the cowl
Cast on 56 sts.
Work in garter stitch (k every row) for 152 rows or until you have almost used up both balls of yarn (leaving enough to sew the ends together).
Bind (cast) off.

Making up and finishing
Twist your knitting once, widthwise.
Sew up the two short ends using flat stitch (see page 25).

Weave in all loose ends.

Simple braided scarf

Skills needed:

- **Cast on**
- **Bind (cast) off**
- **Knit**
- **Purl**
- **Joining seams**
- **Making tassels**

Keep your neck warm when the frost strikes with a giant woolly braid. This super-simple scarf looks like you've worked a fancy cable. But in reality, it's just three long strips braided together. The super-bulky (super-chunky) yarn knits up in a trice, making it an ideal project for beginners who are after something a little different—and for impatient knitters of all levels! I've chosen a delicate shade of cool pale blue for this version, but you can choose any shade you like.

YARN

Lion Brand Wool-Ease Thick & Quick (82% acrylic, 10% wool, 8% rayon) super-bulky (super-chunky) yarn:
 4 x 6oz (170g) balls (106yd/97m) in shade 105 Glacier

NEEDLES AND EQUIPMENT

US size 15 (10mm) knitting needles
Yarn sewing needle

GAUGE (TENSION)

8 sts and 11 rows in stockinette (stocking) stitch to a 4-in (10-cm) square on US size 15 (10mm) needles.

MEASUREMENTS

The finished scarf is 72in (182cm) long and 7in (18cm) wide.

ABBREVIATIONS

k = knit
p = purl
rep = repeat
st st = stockinette (stocking) stitch
st(s) = stitch(es)

For the strips

(make 3)
Cast on 10 sts.
Work in st st as follows:
Row 1: K to end.
Row 2: P to end.
Rep these 2 rows until 170 rows have been worked in total.
Bind (cast) off.

Making up and finishing

Cut 30 12-in (30-cm) lengths of yarn and arrange all but two of the lengths in a neat bunch. Tie one of the yarn lengths securely around the middle point of the bunch. Holding the ends of the tie, smooth the cut edges downward. Tie the second length of yarn around the doubled bunch, about 2in (5cm) from the top. Make a second tassel the same way. Trim the tassel ends.

Lay the three strips on top of each other and oversew the three short ends together. Braid the strips loosely. Lay the three short free ends one on top of the other and oversew the edges together.

Attach the tassels.

Weave in all loose ends.

Bandana Cowl

For an urban take on cute cowboy chic, knit the toddler in your life this neck-warming bandana cowl, complete with subtle spot pattern. I've knitted it in a soft but slightly zingy lime that would suit either a girl or boy—but you can of course knit it in whatever shade takes your fancy. It uses just one ball of yarn, so you may find that you want to knit one to suit every outfit.

Skills needed:

- **Cast on**
- **Bind (cast) off**
- **Knit**
- **Purl**
- **Decreasing**
- **Follow pattern repeats**

YARN

Sublime Baby Cashmerino Silk DK (75% extra fine merino wool, 20% silk, 5% cashmere) light worsted (DK) yarn:
1 x 1¾oz (50g) ball (127yd/116m) in shade 195 Puzzle

NEEDLES AND EQUIPMENT

US size 6 (4mm) knitting needles
Yarn sewing needle

GAUGE (TENSION)

22 sts and 28 rows in stockinette (stocking) stitch to a 4-in (10-cm) square on US size 6 (4mm) needles.

MEASUREMENTS

The bandana cowl is 6½in (16.5cm) wide at the top and 8½in (22cm) long from the neck edge to the pointed lower edge. It should fit an average-size child of 1–3 years.

ABBREVIATIONS
= knit
2tog = knit 2 stitches together
= purl
sso = pass slipped stitch over
m = remain(s)ing
p = repeat
1 = slip 1 stitch
k = slip, slip, knit
(s) = stitch(es)
'S = wrong side
= denotes a sequence of stitches to
e repeated the number of times given
'ter the brackets

or the bandana

ast on 73 sts.
ow 1: K to end.
ow 2: P to end.
ow 3: P1, [k3, p1] to end.
ow 4: P to end.
ow 5: K to end.
ow 6: P to end.
ow 7: K2, p1, [k3, p1] to last 2 sts,
2.
ow 8: P to end.
ow 9: K to end.
ow 10: P to end.
ep rows 3–10 twice more.
ow 27: K20, [p1, k3] 8 times, p1,
20.
ow 28: K19, p35, k to end.
ow 29: K.
ow 30: K19, p35, k to end.
ow 31: Bind (cast) off 16 sts (1 st
em on needle), k5, [p1, k3] 8 times,
3, bind (cast) off rem 16 sts. (41 sts)
reak yarn and rejoin it to WS of
ork.
ow 32: K3, ssk, p to last 5 sts,
2tog, k3. (39 sts)
ow 33: K3, k2tog, k to last 5 sts,
sk, k3. (37 sts)
ow 34: K3, ssk, p to last 5 sts,
2tog, k3. (35 sts)
ow 35: K3, k2tog, [p1, k3] to last 6
ts, p1, ssk, k3. (33 sts)

Rep rows 32–34 once more. (27 sts)
Row 39: K3, k2tog, k2, [p1, k3] to last 8 sts, p1, k2, ssk, k3. (25 sts)
Row 40: K3, p to last 3 sts, k3.
Row 41: K3, k2tog, k to last 5 sts, ssk, k3. (23 sts)
Row 42: K3, p to last 3 sts, k3.
Rep rows 39–42 twice more. (15 sts)
Row 51: K3, k2tog, k2, p1, k2, ssk, k3. (13 sts)
Row 52: K3, p to last 3 sts, k3.
Row 53: K3, k2tog, k3, ssk, k3. (11 sts)
Row 54: K3, p5, k3.
Row 55: K3, k2tog, k1, ssk, k3. (9 sts)
Row 56: K3, p3, k3.
Row 57: K2, k2tog, k1, ssk, k2. (7 sts)
Row 58: K3, p1, k3.

Row 59: K1, k2tog, k1, ssk, k1. (5 sts)
Row 60: K.
Row 61: K2tog, k1, ssk. (3 sts)
Row 62: Sl1, k2tog, psso. (1 st)
Break yarn and fasten off.

Making up and finishing

Sew the back seam of the bandana cowl using mattress stitch (see page 25).

Weave in all loose ends.

CHAPTER 2

Beanies AND Bobble hats

Skills needed:

- **Cast on**
- **Bind (cast) off**
- **Knit**
- **Purl**
- **Follow pattern repeats**
- **Join in new color**
- **Decreasing**
- **Joining seams**

Big and little stripes beanie

Everyone loves a timeless beanie classic—and this one is a dream to make, even for newbie knitters. I've used a soft, light worsted (DK) yarn with a dash of super-soft cashmere—but the pattern would work well in most yarns of this weight, and could be a great yarn stash-buster. Knit it in two colors as I have, or make it plain. Use gentle combinations, or make yourself some dashing rainbow stripes. Rifle through your knitting basket or the shelves of your local yarn store, see what's on offer—and have some fun.

ARN

ublime Baby Cashmere Merino Silk
K (75% extra fine merino, 20% silk, 5%
ashmere) light worsted (DK) yarn:
1 x 1¾oz (50g) ball (127yd/116m) in
shade 277 Tittlemouse (A)
1 x 1¾oz (50g) ball (127yd/116m) in
shade 357 Tiffany (B)

EEDLES AND EQUIPMENT

S size 6 (4mm) knitting needles
arn sewing needle

AUGE (TENSION)

2 sts and 28 rows in stockinette
tocking) stitch to a 4-in (10-cm)
quare on US size 6 (4mm) needles.

EASUREMENTS

he finished hat measures approx.
3½in (34cm) circumference and 10¼in
6cm) high.

BBREVIATIONS

= knit
wise = work as a knit stitch
= purl
2tog = purl 2 stitches together
sso = pass slipped stitch over
2tog = purl 2 sts together
em = remainder
ep = repeat
kpo = slip 1 stitch, knit 1 stitch, pass
lipped stitch over
l = slip
t(s) = stitch(es)
] = denotes a sequence of stitches to
e repeated the number of times given
fter the brackets

or the hat

Cast on 96 sts in A.
Row 1: [K2, p2] to end.
Rep row 1, 15 times more.
Break A and join in B.
Rep row 1, 10 times more.
Leave B at side and join in A.
Rep row 1, 4 times more.

Break A and use B.
Rep row 1, 20 times more.
Break B and work rem of hat in A.
Rep row 1, 14 times more.
Row 65: [K2, p2tog] to end. (72 sts)
Row 66: [K1, p2] to end.
Row 67: [Skpo, p1] to end. (48 sts)
Row 68: [K2, p1] to end.
Row 69: [Sl1 kwise, p1, psso] to end.
(24 sts)
Row 70: [P2tog] to end. (12 sts)
Break yarn, thread it through rem
sts, and pull up securely.

Making up and finishing

Sew the back seam using flat stitch
(see page 25).

Weave in all loose ends.

Fancy rib slouchy beanie

Skills needed:

- **Cast on**
- **Bind (cast) off**
- **Knit**
- **Purl**
- **Decreasing**
- **Follow pattern repeats**
- **Joining seams**

I love the easy-to-knit but rather impressive-looking fancy rib stitch on this slouchy beanie. So if you're after something super-wearable, but just a tiny bit different, why not give it a go? The alpaca in the wool-mix yarn gives it a luxurious feel, and it's also super-comfy and hardwearing. The denim shade is great because it goes with practically everything, but as usual, the color is entirely up to you.

YARN
Katia Peru (40% wool, 40% acrylic, 20% alpaca) bulky (chunky) yarn:
  2 x 3½oz (100g) balls (116yd/106m) in shade 18 Light Denim

NEEDLES AND EQUIPMENT
US size 10½ (6.5mm) knitting needles
Yarn sewing needle

GAUGE (TENSION)
12 sts and 16 rows in stockinette (stocking) stitch to a 4-in (10-cm) square using US size 10½ (6.5mm) needles.

MEASUREMENTS
The finished hat measures approx. 18in (46cm) circumference and 12in (30cm) high.

ABBREVIATIONS
k = knit
k2tog = knit 2 stitches together
p = purl
p2tog = purl 2 stitches together
rep = repeat
sk2po = slip 1 stitch, knit 2 stitches, pass slipped stitch over
st(s) = stitch(es)
[ ] = denotes a sequence of stitches to be repeated the number of times given after the brackets

For the hat
Cast on 71 sts.
Row 1: [K2, p2] to last 3 sts, k2, p1.
Rep row 1, 47 times more.
Row 49: K1, [sk2po, k1] 17 times, k2tog. (36 sts)
Row 50: [K1, p1] to end.
Row 51: K1, [k2tog] to last st, k1. (19 sts)
Row 52: P1, [p2tog] to end. (10 sts)
Break yarn, thread it through rem sts, and pull up securely.

Making up and finishing
Sew the back seam using flat stitch (see page 25).

Weave in all loose ends.

Multicolored bobble beret

This traditional beret is perfect for all ages, and will work just as well whether you're dressing up or dressing down. It's knitted entirely in stockinette (stocking) stitch, so is a perfect second or third project for new knitters who are ready to tackle a bit of decreasing. And the multicolored yarn is a godsend, as it means you can create lovely stripes without the hassle of changing yarns. I've added a coordinating pompom to this version—but it would look good plain as well.

Skills needed:

- **Cast on**
- **Bind (cast) off**
- **Knit**
- **Purl**
- **Increasing**
- **Decreasing**
- **Joining seams**
- **Making pompoms**

YARN

Lion Brand Unique (100% acrylic) bulky (chunky) yarn:
  1 x 3½oz (100g) ball (109yd/100m) in shade 200 Harvest (A)
Debbie Bliss Cashmerino Aran (55% wool, 33% acrylic, 12% cashmere) worsted (Aran) yarn:
  1 x 1¾oz (50g) ball (98yd/90m) in shade 502 Lime (B)

NEEDLES AND EQUIPMENT

US size 9 (5.5mm) knitting needles
Yarn sewing needle
Pompom maker to make 2¾in (7cm) pompom, or two cardboard circles each measuring 2¾in (7cm) in diameter with a 1¼in (3cm) diameter hole in the center.

GAUGE (TENSION)

15 sts and 20 rows in stockinette (stocking) stitch to a 4-in (10-cm) square on US size 9 (5.5mm) needles.

MEASUREMENTS

The finished beret measures approx. 18in (46cm) circumference, 11in (28cm) diameter.

BBREVIATIONS

eg = beginning

= knit

2tog = knit 2 stitches together

1 = make 1

= purl

2tog = purl 2 stitches together

ep = repeat

k2po = slip 1 stitch, knit 2 stitches,
ass slipped stitch over

:(s) = stitch(es)

: st = stockinette (stocking) stitch

| = denotes a sequence of stitches to
e repeated the number of times given
fter the brackets

or the beret

ast on 72 sts in A.

ow 1: [K1, p1] to end.

ep row 1, 5 times more.

ow 7: K3, [m1, k6] 11 times, m1, k3.
34 sts)

eg with a p row, work 17 rows in
t st.

ow 25: K6, [k2tog, k12] 5 times,
2tog, k6. (78 sts)

eg with a p row, work 3 rows in
t st.

ow 29: K5, [sk2po, k10] 5 times,
k2po, k5. (66 sts)

eg with a p row, work 3 rows in
t st.

ow 33: K4, [sk2po, k8] 5 times,
k2po, k4. (54 sts)

eg with a p row, work 3 rows in
t st.

ow 37: K3, [sk2po, k6] 5 times,
k2po, k3. (42 sts)

eg with a p row, work 3 rows in
t st.

ow 41: K2, [sk2po, k4] 5 times,
k2po, k2. (30 sts)

ow 42: P.

ow 43: K1, [sk2po, k2] 5 times,
k2po, k1. (18 sts)

ow 44: [P2tog] to end. (9 sts)

3reak yarn, thread it through rem
sts, and pull up securely.

Making up and finishing

Sew the back seam using mattress
stitch (see page 25). Using the
pompom maker or cardboard
circles (see page 27), make a
pompom in B. Trim the pompom
and use the tails of yarn to sew it to
the center of the beret.

Weave in all loose ends.

The finished beret will need a
quick spray and shape (see page
17), to give it its finished shape.

Stitch-pattern slouchy beanie

I've given this texture-stripe beanie a subtle twist by adding a super-soft alpaca border with a little turned-up edge. The main part of the hat is a tad more classic and is perfect for cool mornings and evenings that sometimes call for a hat—but not one that's too serious.

Skills needed:

- **Cast on**
- **Bind (cast) off**
- **Knit**
- **Purl**
- **Decreasing**
- **Follow pattern repeats**
- **Join in a new color**
- **Joining seams**

YARN

Rowan Alpaca Color (100% alpaca) light worsted (DK) yarn:
  1 x 1¾oz (50g) ball (131yd/120m) in shade 138 Ruby (A)
Cascade 220 Superwash (100% wool) worsted (Aran) yarn:
  1 x 3½oz (100g) ball (220yd/200m) in shade 1940 Peach (B)

NEEDLES AND EQUIPMENT

US size 5 (3.75mm) knitting needles
US size 6 (4mm) knitting needles
Yarn sewing needle

GAUGE (TENSION)

22 sts and 30 rows in stockinette (stocking) stitch to a 4-in (10-cm) square on US size 6 (4mm) needles.

MEASUREMENTS

The finished hat measures approx. 17in (44cm) circumference and 9½in (24cm) high.

ABBREVIATIONS

beg = beginning
k = knit
p = purl
p2tog = purl 2 stitches together
rep = repeat
sk2po = slip 1 stitch, knit 2 stitches, pass slipped stitch over
st(s) = stitch(es)
st st = stockinette (stocking) stitch
[ ] = denotes a sequence of stitches to be repeated the number of times given after the brackets

For the hat

Using US size 5 (3.75mm) needles, cast on 102 sts in A.

Beg with a k row, work 4 rows in st st.

Row 5: K2, [p2, k2] to end.

Row 6: P2, [k2, p2] to end.

Rows 7–10: Rep rows 5–6 twice more. Break A, join in B and change to US size 6 (4mm) needles.

Beg with a k row, work 6 rows in st st.

Beg with a p row, work 6 rows in st st.

Rep last 12 rows, 3 times more.

Beg with a k row, work 2 rows in st st.

Row 61: K7, [sk2po, k14] 5 times, sk2po, k7. (90 sts)

Row 62: P.

Row 63: K6, [sk2po, k12] 5 times, sk2po, k6. (78 sts)

Row 64: P.

Row 65: K5, [sk2po, k10] 5 times, sk2po, k5. (66 sts)

Row 66: P.

Row 67: K4, [sk2po, k8] 5 times, sk2po, k4. (54 sts)

Row 68: P.

Row 69: K3, [sk2po, k6] 5 times, sk2po, k3. (42 sts)

Row 70: P.

Row 71: K2, [sk2po, k4] 5 times, sk2po, k2. (30 sts)

Row 72: P.

Row 73: K1, [sk2po, k2] 5 times, sk2po, k1. (18 sts)

Row 74: [P2tog] to end. (9 sts)

Break yarn, thread it through rem sts, and pull up securely.

Making up and finishing

Sew the back seam using mattress stitch (see page 25).

Weave in all loose ends.

Skills needed:

- Cast on
- Bind (cast) off
- Knit
- Purl
- Decreasing
- Follow pattern repeats
- Joining seams
- Making pompoms

Simple knit bobble hat

Sometimes, the simple things in life really are the best—and I think this super-chunky, super-quick hat is one of them. Knitted mostly in garter stitch and with just some simple decreasing, it's well within the grasp of the newest of new knitters—and an intermediate knitter could probably finish it in just an evening or two. So now you have no excuses. Choose your yarn—I've chosen a lovely soft ice blue—grab your needles… and go.

YARN

Lion Brand Wool-Ease Thick & Quick (80% acrylic, 20% wool) super-bulky (super-chunky) yarn:

   1 x 6oz (170g) ball (108yd/98m) in shade 105 Glacier (A)

Sirdar Big Softie (51% wool, 49% acrylic) super-bulky (super-chunky) yarn:

   1 x 1¾oz (50g) ball (49yd/45m) in shade 321 Beanie (B)

NEEDLES AND EQUIPMENT

US size 13 (9mm) knitting needles
US size 15 (10mm) knitting needles
Yarn sewing needle
Pompom maker to make 4½in (11.5cm) pompom, or two cardboard circles each measuring 4½in (11.5cm) in diameter with a 2¼in (5.5cm) diameter hole in the center

GAUGE (TENSION)

9 sts and 12 rows in stockinette (stocking) stitch to a 4-in (10-cm) square on US size 15 (10mm) needles.

MEASUREMENTS

The finished hat measures approx. 20in (50cm) circumference and 10in (25cm) high.

ABBREVIATIONS

k = knit
k2tog = knit 2 stitches together
p = purl
rem = remaining
rep = repeat
sk2po = slip 1 stitch, knit 2 stitches, pass slipped stitch over
st(s) = stitch(es)
[ ] = denotes a sequence of stitches to be repeated the number of times given after the brackets

For the hat

Using US size 13 (9mm) needles, cast on 54 sts in A.
Row 1: [K1, p1] to end.
Rep row 1, 3 times more.
Change to US size 15 (10mm) needles.
K 24 rows.
Row 29: K3, [sk2po, k6] 5 times, sk2po, k3. (42 sts)

Row 30: K.
Row 31: K2, [sk2po, k4] 5 times, sk2po, k2. (30 sts)
Row 32: [K2tog] to end. (15 sts)
Row 33: [K2tog] 3 times, k3, [k2tog] 3 times. (9 sts)
Break yarn, thread it through rem sts, and pull up securely.

Making up and finishing

Sew the back seam using flat stitch (see page 25).

Using the pompom maker or cardboard circles (see page 27), make a pompom winding A and B together, using A to tie round the pompom center. Trim the pompom and use the tails of yarn to sew it to the top of the hat.

Weave in all loose ends.

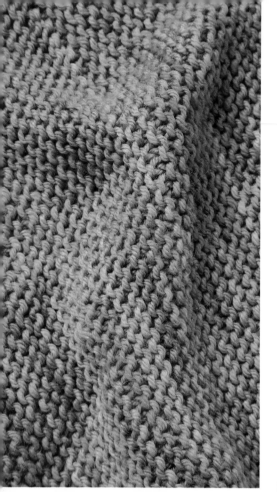

Self-striped slouchy beanie

This side-knitted beanie is one of my favorites, though I'm not sure exactly why. It could be the way the hat shapes itself from the beginning. Or it could be the beautiful simplicity of the stitch. Or perhaps it's the fabulous multicolor yarn that creates a unique pattern as you knit—check out the yarn range to see the amazing selection on offer. I just know that I love it, and I hope you will, too.

Skills needed:

- **Cast on**
- **Bind (cast) off**
- **Knit**
- **Wrapping the yarn**
- **Joining seams**

YARN

Cascade 220 Superwash Paints (100% wool) worsted (Aran) yarn:
  1 x 3½oz (100g) ball (220yd/200m) in shade 9791 Rainbow Sherbert

NEEDLES AND EQUIPMENT

US size 6 (4mm) knitting needles
Yarn sewing needle

GAUGE (TENSION)

22 sts and 22 rows in stockinette (stocking) stitch to a 4-in (10-cm) square on US size 6 (4mm) needles.

MEASUREMENTS

The finished hat measures approx. 16in (40cm) circumference and 10½in (27cm) high.

ABBREVIATIONS

k = knit
rep = repeat
st(s) = stitch(es)
WT = wrap and turn: with yarn at the back, slip the next stitch purlwise from the left-hand to the right-hand needle. Bring the yarn forward between the needles. Slip the stitch from the right-hand needle back to the left-hand needle. Take the yarn back between the needles. Turn the work.

For the hat

Cast on 48 sts.
Row 1: K.
Row 2: K47, WT.
Row 3: K.
Row 4: K45, WT.
Row 5: K.
Row 6: K43, WT.

Row 7: K.
Row 8: K41, WT.
Row 9: K.
Row 10: K39, WT.
Row 11: K.
Row 12: K37, WT.
Row 13: K.
Row 14: K35, WT.
Row 15: K.

Row 16: K33, WT.
Row 17: K.
Row 18: K31, WT.
Row 19: K.
Rows 20–21: K 2 rows.
Rep rows 1–21, 5 times
more.
Rep rows 1–19 once more.
Bind (cast) off.

Making up and finishing

Sew the back seam using flat stitch
(see page 25).

Weave in all loose ends.

Three-color bobble hat

Sometimes, only something classically simple will fit the bill. So here is a traditional bobble hat that you can customize to your own style. Knit it in two colors and add a bobble in another color—just like I have. Knit it totally plain. Or knit it in stripes. I've chosen a lovely cotton-rich yarn for this hat, so you can keep it to hand to ward off any cool spring breezes. And it's chunky, so it will knit up in just an evening or two.

Skills needed:

- **Cast on**
- **Bind (cast) off**
- **Knit**
- **Purl**
- **Decreasing**
- **Follow pattern repeats**
- **Join in a new color**
- **Joining seams**
- **Making pompoms**

YARN
Rowan All Seasons Chunky (60% cotton, 40% acrylic) bulky (chunky) yarn:
  1 x 3½oz (100g) ball (93yd/85m) in shade 609 Jetsam (A)
  1 x 3½oz (100g) ball (93yd/85m) in shade 603 Drift (B)
  1 x 3½oz (100g) ball (93yd/85m) in shade 611 Samphire (C)

NEEDLES AND EQUIPMENT
US size 10½ (6.5mm) knitting needles
Yarn sewing needle
Pompom maker to make 2¾in (7cm) pompom, or two cardboard circles each measuring 2¾in (7cm) in diameter with a 1¼in (3cm) diameter hole in the center

GAUGE (TENSION)
14 sts and 16 rows in stockinette (stocking) stitch to a 4-in (10-cm) square on US size 10½ (6.5mm) needles.

MEASUREMENTS
The finished hat measures approx. 20in (50cm) circumference and 8¼in (21cm) high excluding the pompom.

ABBREVIATIONS
beg = beginning
k = knit
k2tog = knit 2 stitches together
p = purl
p2sso = pass 2 slipped stitches over
rem = remaining
rep = repeat
sl2 = slip 2 stitches

st st = stockinette (stocking) stitch

st(s) = stitch(es)

[ ] = denotes a sequence of stitches to be repeated the number of times given after the brackets

For the hat

Cast on 60 sts in A.

Row 1: [K2, p2] to end.

Rep row 1, 5 times more.

Break A and join in B.

Work 20 rows in st st beg with a k row.

Row 27: K4, [k2tog, k8] 5 times, k2tog, k4. (54 sts)

Row 28: P.

Row 29: K3, [sl2, k1, p2sso, k6] 5 times, sl2, k1, p2sso, k3.

Row 30: P.

Row 31: K2, [sl2, k1, p2sso, k4] 5 times, sl2, k1, p2sso, k2.

Row 32: P.

Row 33: K1, [sl2, k1, p2sso, k2] 5 times, sl2, k1, p2sso, k1.

Row 34: P.

Row 35: [Sl2, k1, p2sso] 6 times. Break yarn, thread it through rem sts, and pull up securely.

Making up and finishing

Sew the back seam using mattress stitch (see page 25).

Using the pompom maker or cardboard circles (see page 27), make a pompom using C. Trim the pompom and use the tails of yarn to sew it to the top of the hat.

Weave in all loose ends.

Bow beanie

Pretty as a picture, this 1920s-inspired hat is made from a cotton mix yarn—so it's the ideal head warmer for those early days of spring, when you don't need something too warm and fuzzy. The yarn is available in a range of pretty sherbet shades—I've chosen pale green and the palest of yellows, but you can create your beanie in any shade you want. And if you're after something just a little less girly, simply omit the bow. The hat is worked exclusively in knit and purl stitches, so is an ideal early project for the new knitter.

Skills needed:

- **Cast on**
- **Bind (cast) off**
- **Knit**
- **Purl**
- **Decreasing**
- **Follow pattern repeats**
- **Join in a new color**
- **Joining seams**

YARN
Lion Brand Baby's First (55% acrylic, 45% cotton) bulky (chunky) yarn:
  1 x 3½oz (100g) ball (120yd/110m) in shade 156 Beanstalk (A)
  1 x 3½oz (100g) ball (120yd/110m) in shade 099 Pixie Dust (B)

NEEDLES AND EQUIPMENT
US size 10 (6mm) knitting needles
Yarn sewing needle

GAUGE (TENSION)
12 sts and 18 rows in stockinette (stocking) stitch to a 4-in (10-cm) square on US size 10 (6mm) needles.

MEASUREMENTS
The finished hat measures approx. 16½in (42cm) circumference and 7½in (19cm) high. It should fit an average-size child of 5–10 years.

ABBREVIATIONS
k = knit
k2tog = knit 2 stitches together
p = purl
p2sso = pass 2 slipped stitches over
p2tog = purl 2 stitches together
rem = remaining
rep = repeat
sl2 = slip 2 stitches
ssk = slip, slip, knit
st st = stockinette (stocking) stitch
st(s) = stitch(es)
[ ] = denotes a sequence of stitches to be repeated the number of times given after the brackets

Row 29: K2, [sl2, k1, p2sso, k4] 5 times, sl2, k1, p2sso, k2. (30 sts)

Row 30: P.

Row 31: K1, [sl2, k1, p2sso, k2] 5 times, sl2, k1, p2sso, k1. (18 sts)

Row 32: [P2tog] to end. (9 sts)

Row 31: [K2tog] twice, k1, [ssk] twice. (5 sts)

Break yarn, thread it through rem sts, and pull up securely.

For the bow

Main part

Cast on 9 sts in B.

Beg with a k row, work 20 rows in st st.

Bind (cast) off.

Center

Cast on 3 sts in B.

Beg with a k row, work 6 rows in st st.

Bind (cast) off.

Making up and finishing

Sew the back seam using flat stitch (see page 25).

Wrap the bow center around the middle of the bow, remembering that the front side of the bow is the "reverse" side of the stockinette (stocking) stitch. Sew the bow in place on the center of the band on the hat.

Weave in all loose ends.

For the hat

Cast on 60 sts in A.

Row 1: [K2, p2] to end.

Rep row 1, 3 times more.

Row 5: K.

Row 6: P.

Leave A at side and join in B.

Beg with a k row, work 4 rows in st st.

Break B and work rem of main hat in A.

Beg with a k row, work 14 rows in st st.

Row 25: K4, [k2tog, k8] 5 times, k2tog, k4. (54 sts)

Row 26: P.

Row 27: K3, [sl2, k1, p2sso, k6] 5 times, sl2, k1, p2sso, k3. (42 sts)

Row 28: P.

Tricolor bobble hat

If you're after a contemporary, nautical twist on the most classic of bobble hats, look no further. This striped hat with its distinctive red bobble is knitted in a baby-soft merino yarn in straightforward stockinette (stocking) stitch. It's simple enough to suit novice knitters and is an ideal project for those keen to dip their toes into the world of two-color knitting.

Skills needed:

- **Cast on**
- **Bind (cast) off**
- **Knit**
- **Purl**
- **Decreasing**
- **Follow pattern repeats**
- **Join in a new color**
- **Joining seams**
- **Making pompoms**

YARN

Sublime Extra Fine Merino DK (100% extra fine merino wool) light worsted (DK) yarn:

   1 x 1¾oz (50g) ball (127yd/116m) in shade 015 Clipper (A)
   1 x 1¾oz (50g) ball (127yd/116m) in shade 307 Julep (B)
   1 x 1¾oz (50g) ball (127yd/116m) in shade 167 Red Hot (C)

NEEDLES AND EQUIPMENT

US size 5 (3.75mm) knitting needles
US size 6 (4mm) knitting needles
Yarn sewing needle
Pompom maker to make 2¾in (7cm) pompom, or two cardboard circles each measuring 2¾in (7cm) in diameter with a 1¼in (3cm) diameter hole in the center

GAUGE (TENSION)

22 sts and 28 rows in stockinette (stocking) stitch to a 4-in (10-cm) square on US size 6 (4mm) needles.

MEASUREMENTS

The finished hat measures approx. 15in (38cm) circumference and 8in (20cm) high, excluding pompom. It should fit an average-size child of 5–10 years.

ABBREVIATIONS

k = knit
p = purl
p2sso = pass 2 slipped stitches over
rem = remaining
rep = repeat
sl2 = slip 2 stitches
st st = stockinette (stocking) stitch
st(s) = stitch(es)
[ ] = denotes a sequence of stitches to be repeated the number of times given after the brackets

For the hat

Using US size 5 (3.75mm) needles, cast on 102 sts in A.

Row 1: [K3, p3] to end.

Rep row 1, 13 times more.

Leave A at side, join in B and change to US size 6 (4mm) needles.

Row 15: K.

Row 16: P.

Leave B at side and use A.

Row 17: K.

Row 18: P.

Rep rows 15–18, 7 times more.

Leave A at side and use B.

Row 47: K7, [sl2, k1, p2sso, k14] 5 times, sl2, k1, p2sso, k7. (90 sts)

Row 48: P.

Leave B at side and use A.

Row 49: K6, [sl2, k1, p2sso, k12] 5 times, sl2, k1, p2sso, k6. (78 sts)

Row 50: P.

Leave A at side and use B.

Row 51: K5, [sl2, k1, psso, k10] 5 times, sl2, k1, p2sso, k5. (66 sts)

Row 52: P.

Leave B at side and use A.

Row 53: K4, [sl2, k1, psso, k8] 5 times, sl2, k1, p2sso, k4. (54 sts)

Row 54: P.

Leave A at side and use B.

Row 55: K3, [sl2, k1, p2sso, k6] 5 times, sl2, k1, p2sso, k3. (42 sts)

Row 56: P.

Leave B at side and use A.

Row 57: K2, [sl2, k1, p2sso, k4] 5 times, sl2, k1, p2sso, k2. (30 sts)

Row 58: P.

Break A and use B.

Row 59: K1, [sl2, k1, p2sso, k2] 5 times, sl2, k1, p2sso, k1. (18 sts)

Row 60: [P2tog] to end. (9 sts)

Break yarn, thread it through rem sts, and pull up securely.

Making up and finishing

Sew the back seam using mattress stitch (see page 25).

Using the pompom maker or cardboard circles (see page 27), make a pompom in C. Trim the pompom and use the tails of yarn to sew it to the top of the hat.

Weave in all loose ends.

CHAPTER 3

FOR THE *Home*

Bunting

These days, bunting isn't just for street parties and big outdoor occasions—you can use it to celebrate whatever you want, in your own home. This easy-to-knit bunting is the perfect way for newbie knitters to make their mark on the world of interior decorating. Go pastel sweet as shown here, or choose your own riot of colors. Go short, go long—the decision is entirely down to you.

Skills needed:

- **Cast on**
- **Bind (cast) off**
- **Knit**
- **Purl**
- **Decreasing**
- **Joining seams**
- **Crochet chain**

YARN

Sublime Baby Cashmere Merino Silk DK (75% extra fine merino wool, 20% silk, 5% cashmere) light worsted (DK) yarn:

 1 x 1¾ oz/50g ball (127yd/116m) each in shades 195 Puzzle, 162 Pinkaboo, 048 Cheeky (A)

Patons Diploma Gold DK (55% wool, 25% acrylic, 20% nylon) light worsted (DK) yarn:

 Small amount of shade 6142 Cream (B)

NEEDLES AND EQUIPMENT

US size 3 (3.25mm) knitting needles
Yarn sewing needle
Size G6 (4mm) or similar size crochet hook
Small safety pin

GAUGE (TENSION)

27 sts and 36 rows in stockinette (stocking) stitch to a 4-in (10-cm) square on US size 3 (3.25mm) needles.

MEASUREMENTS

Each pennant measures 4in (10cm) from base to tip. The bunting has 9 pennants threaded on a 60-in (1.5m) cord.

ABBREVIATIONS

k = knit
k2tog = knit 2 stitches together
p = purl
rem = remaining
rep = repeat
RS = right side
ssk = slip, slip, knit
st(s) = stitch(es)
WS = wrong side

Row 11: K2, p to last 2 sts, k2.
Rep Rows 8–11 twice more. (20 sts)
Row 20: K1, ssk, k to last 3 sts, k2tog, k1. (18 sts)
Row 21: K2, p to last 2 sts, k2.
Rep Rows 20–21 six times more. (6 sts)
Row 34: K1, ssk, k2tog, k1. (4 sts)
Row 35: K.
Row 36: Ssk, k2tog. (2 sts)
Row 37: K.
Row 38: K2tog. (1 st)
Break yarn and pull through rem st.

For the cord
Using the crochet hook and B, make a 60-in (1.5-m) crochet chain (see page 26 for instructions).

Making up and finishing
Weave in loose yarn ends at the tips of the Pennants and the ends of the crocheted Cord.

With the RS of the Pennants facing, fold over the base of each Pennant to the WS and oversew in place using matching color A to form the casing for the Cord.

Using the safety pin, thread the Cord through the casings of the Pennants, alternating colors as you go. Spread the Pennants out evenly on the Cord, leaving sufficient length free at each end for hanging up your bunting.

For the pennants
(make 3 in each color A)
Cast on 26 sts.
K 4 rows.
Row 5: K2, p to last 2 sts, k2.
Row 6: K.
Row 7: K2, p to last 2 sts, k2.
Row 8: K1, ssk, k to last 3 sts, k2tog, k1. (24 sts)
Row 9: K2, p to last 2 sts, k2.
Row 10: K.

Striped pillow

With some thick pure-wool yarn and a pair of big knitting needles, you can create a sophisticated pillow cover in no time. The cover features some simple but lovely textures and is made from three rectangles, with no tricky fastenings. There is a simple vent at the back for inserting your pillow form (and removing it if you want to wash the cover) and it is finished off with natural mother-of-pearl buttons for that extra touch of class.

Skills needed:

- Cast on
- Bind (cast) off
- Knit
- Purl
- Follow pattern repeats
- Join in a new color

YARN

Rowan Big Wool (100% wool) super-bulky (super-chunky) yarn:
  2 x 3½oz/100g balls (174yd/160m) in shade 061 Concrete (A)
  1 x 3½oz/100g ball (87yd/80m) each in shades 068 Sun (B), 001 White Hot (C)

NEEDLES AND EQUIPMENT

US size 10½ (6.5mm) knitting needles
Yarn sewing needle
Standard sewing needle

OTHER MATERIALS

4 x ¾in (2cm) mother-of-pearl buttons
Standard white sewing thread
12 x 20in (30 x 50cm) pillow form

GAUGE (TENSION)

11 sts and 16 rows in stockinette (stocking) stitch to a 4-in (10cm) square on US size 10½ (6.5mm) needles.

MEASUREMENTS

To fit a 12 x 20in (30 x 50cm) pillow form.

ABBREVIATIONS

k = knit
p = purl
rep = repeat
RS = right side
st st = stockinette (stocking) stitch
st(s) = stitch(es)
WS = wrong side
[ ] = denotes a sequence of stitches to be repeated the number of times given after the brackets

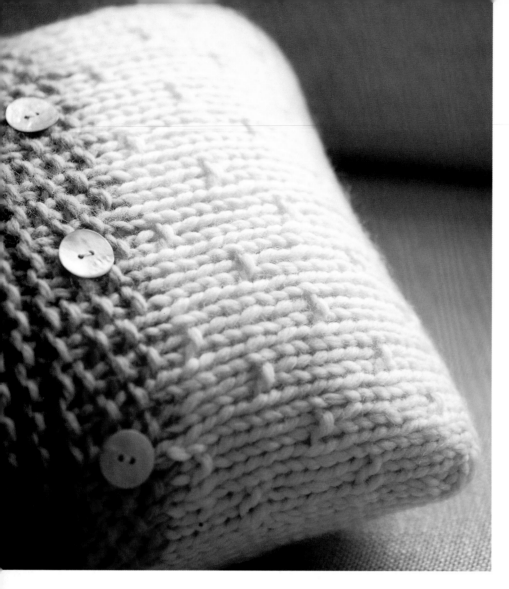

Work 3 rows in st st beg with a p row.
Bind (cast) off.

Back Piece 1
(make 1)
Cast on 33 sts in B.
Work 38 rows in st st beg with a k row.
Bind (cast) off.

Back Piece 2
(make 1)
Cast on 33 sts in C.
Work 37 rows in st st beg with a k row.
Next row: K.
Bind (cast) off.

Making up and finishing
Weave in all loose ends.

Lay the Front RS down. Lay the Piece 1 RS up on the WS of the Fron and join along the three matching edges using mattress stitch (see page 25) and A.

With the Front still RS down, lay Piece 2 on top so it overlaps Piece 1 across the middle of the pillow cover to form a flap to insert the pillow form. Sew Piece 2 to the Front along the three matching edges using mattress stitch.

Sew the buttons in place along the stripe in B on the front of the pillow Insert the pillow form.

For the pillow cover
Front
(make 1)
Cast on 33 sts in A.
Rows 1–60: K.
Break A and join in B.
Row 61: K.
Row 62: K1, [p1, k1] to end.
Rep last row 4 times more.
Break B and join in C.
Work 2 rows in st st beg with a k row.
Row 69: K4, [p1, k3] to last st, k1.
Work 3 rows in st st beg with a p row.
Row 73: K2, [p1, k3] to last 3 sts, p1, k2.
Work 3 rows in st st beg with a p row.
Rep last 8 rows once more.
Row 85: K4, [p1, k3] to last st, k1.

Potholder

Add a touch of retro charm to your kitchen with this charming potholder. Knitted quite tightly in a chunky wool yarn in the palest of blues, it offers excellent protection from those hot pot handles. It will look good, too, hanging in your kitchen. The potholder is an excellent project if you're new to knitting—especially if you're the sort of person who wants something practical as well as decorative.

Skills needed:

● **Cast on** ● **Bind (cast) off** ● **Knit** ● **Purl** ● **Follow pattern repeats**

YARN
Rowan Big Wool (100% wool) super-bulky (super- chunky) yarn:
  1 x 3½oz/100g ball (87yd/80m) in shade 021 Ice Blue

NEEDLES AND EQUIPMENT
US size 8 (5mm) knitting needles
Yarn sewing needle

GAUGE (TENSION)
14 sts and 22 rows in main pattern to a 4-in (10-cm) square on US size 8 (5mm) needles.

MEASUREMENTS
The potholder measures 8¾in (22cm) square, excluding loop.

ABBREVIATIONS
k = knit
p = purl
rep = repeat
st(s) = stitch(es)
[ ] = denotes a sequence of stitches to be repeated the number of times given after the brackets

For the potholder
Main piece
(make 1)
Cast on 33 sts.
K 4 rows.
Row 5: K6, [p1, k1, p1, k3] to last 3 sts, k3.
Row 6: K3, p4, k1, [p5, k1] to last 7 sts, p4, k3.
Rep last 2 rows 19 times more.
Row 45: K6, [p1, k1, p1, k3] to last 3 sts, k3.
K 3 rows.
Bind (cast) off.

For the loop
(make 1)
Cast on 22 sts.
Bind (cast) off.

Making up and finishing
Use the two yarn tails on the Loop to sew it to one corner of the Main Piece.

Weave in any other loose ends.

Bolster

At the end of the day when you want to settle into your favorite seat and put your feet up, this bolster cushion is the icing on the cake. Knitted in a retro-style wave pattern, it's a great first project for knitters getting used to working with two colors at a time—and the super-chunky yarn and super-chunky needles to match mean it will be ready in almost no time.

Skills needed:

- **Cast on**
- **Bind (cast) off**
- **Knit**
- **Purl**
- **Decreasing**
- **Increasing**
- **Follow pattern repeats**
- **Join in a new color**
- **Joining seams**

YARN

Rowan Big Wool (100% merino wool) super-bulky (super-chunky) yarn:
   1 x 3½oz/100g ball (87yd/80m) in each of shades 036 Glamour (A), 064 Prize (B), 068 Sun (C), 001 Hot White (D)

NEEDLES AND EQUIPMENT

Size US size 10½ (6.5mm) knitting needles
Yarn sewing needle

OTHER MATERIALS

18in (46cm) x 8in (20cm) diameter bolster pillow form

GAUGE (TENSION)

12 sts and 15 rows in stockinette (stocking) stitch to a 4-in (10-cm) square on US size 10½ (6.5mm) needles.

MEASUREMENTS

To fit an 18in (46cm) x 8in (20cm) diameter bolster pillow form.

ABBREVIATIONS

beg = beginning
cont = continue
inc1 = increase 1 stitch
k = knit
k2tog = knit 2 stitches together
p = purl
pwise = work as a purl stitch
rep = repeat
RS = right side
ssk = slip, slip, knit
st st = stockinette (stocking) stitch
st(s) = stitch(es)
[ ] = denotes a sequence of stitches to be repeated the number of times given after the brackets

Cont in D only.
Beg with a p row, cont in st st until
work measures 17¾in (45cm),
ending with a p row.
Bind (cast) off.

End pieces
(make 2)
Cast on 12 sts in D.
Row 1: Inc1, k to last st, inc1, k1. (1⁴
sts)
Row 2: P.
Rep last 2 rows 4 times more. (22
sts)
Work 10 rows in st st beg with a k
row.
Row 21: K1, k2tog, k to last 3 sts,
ssk, k1. (20 sts)
Row 22: P.
Rep last 2 rows 3 times more. (14
sts)
Row 29: K1, k2tog, k to last 3 sts,
ssk, k1. (12 sts)
Bind (cast) off pwise.

For the bolster
Main piece
(make 1)
Cast on 71 sts in A.
Work 6 rows in st st beg with a k
row.
Row 7: K1 in B, [k4 in A, k1 in B] to
end.
Row 8: P1 in B, [p4 in A, p1 in B] to
end.
Row 9: K2 in B, [k2 in A, k3 in B] to
last 4 sts, k2 in A, k2 in B.
Break A.
Work 3 rows in st st beg with a p
row.

Row 13: K1 in C, [k4 in B, k1 in C] to
end.
Row 14: P1 in C, [p4 in B, p1 in C] to
end.
Row 15: K2 in C, [k2 in B, k3 in C] to
last 4 sts, k2 in B, k2 in C.
Break B.
Work 3 rows in st st beg with a p
row.
Row 19: K1 in D, [k4 in C, k1 in D] to
end.
Row 20: P1 in D, [p4 in C, p1 in D] to
end.
Row 21: K2 in D, [k2 in C, k3 in D] to
last 4 sts, k2 in C, k2 in D.
Break C.

Making up and finishing
Weave in all loose ends.

Join seam of Main Piece using
mattress stitch (see page 25),
leaving a 7-in (17.5-cm) gap in the
center for inserting the pillow form.
From the RS, join the End Pieces
in place using mattress stitch so
that the cast-on and bound-(cast-)
off edges of the main piece form
a narrow border round the
circumference of the end pieces.
Insert the pillow form and close the
gap using mattress stitch.

Tablet cozy

Keep your treasured tablet safe and sound in its own stripy home. This is one of the simplest projects in the book to knit, and an ideal second or third project for the newbie knitter. As a bonus, it is also very straightforward to seam together. Why not make it as a gift in the colors of the lucky recipient's favorite sports team?

Skills needed:

- **Cast on**
- **Bind (cast) off**
- **Knit**
- **Purl**
- **Decreasing**
- **Follow pattern repeats**
- **Join in a new color**
- **Joining seams**

YARN

Rowan Wool Cotton DK (50% merino wool, 50% cotton) light worsted (DK) yarn:

1 x 1¾oz/50g ball (123½yd/113m) in each of shades 943 Flower (A) and 946 Elf (B)

NEEDLES AND EQUIPMENT

US size 8 (5mm) knitting needles
Yarn sewing needle

OTHER MATERIALS

1in (2.5cm) green button

GAUGE (TENSION)

15 sts and 24 rows in stockinette (stocking) stitch to a 4-in (10-cm) square on US size 8 (5 mm) needles, using yarn double. **Note:** you will need to rewind your yarn into two smaller balls, hold the yarn from each ball together in your hand, and knit with both strands at the same time.

MEASUREMENTS

Laid flat the case measures 7¾ x 10in (19.5 x 25cm), to fit a tablet measuring approx. 7¼ x 9½in (18.5 x 24cm). The case will fit the tablet quite snugly, which will help keep it secure.

ABBREVIATIONS

beg = beginning
k = knit
kwise = work as a knit stitch
k2tog = knit 2 stitches together
p = purl
rep = repeat
ssk = slip, slip, knit
st st = stockinette (stocking) stitch
st(s) = stitch(es)
WS = wrong side
[ ] = denotes a sequence of stitches to be repeated the number of times given after the brackets

For the cozy

Front/back

(make 2 the same)

Cast on 32 sts in A, using yarn double; see Note under Gauge (Tension) on page 89.

Rows 1–6: Work in st st beg with a k row.

Leaving A at side, join in a doubled strand of B.

Rows 7–8: Work in st st beg with a k row.

Rep last 8 rows 5 times more.

Fasten off B.

Work 2 rows in st st using A.

Row 51: [K2, p2] to end.

Rep last row twice more.

Bind (cast) off kwise.

Flap

Cast on 32 sts in A, using yarn double.

Row 1: K.

Row 2: K3, p to last 3 sts, k3.

Rep last 2 rows 3 times more.

Row 9: K1, k2tog, k to last 3 sts, ssk, k1. (30 sts)

Row 10: K3, p to last 3 sts, k3.

Row 11: K.

Row 12: K3, p to last 3 sts, k3.

Row 13: K1, k2tog, k to last 3 sts, ssk, k1. (28 sts)

Row 14: K1, k2tog, k9, bind (cast) of 4 sts (for the buttonhole), k to last 3 sts, ssk, k1. (22 sts)

Row 15: K1, k2tog, k8, turn work and cast on 4 sts (for the buttonhole), turn work again, k to last 3 sts, ssk, k1. (24 sts)

Row 16: K1, k2tog, k to last 3 sts, ssk, k1. (22 sts)

Bind (cast) off.

Making up and finishing

Weave in all loose ends.

With WS together, join the Front and Back of the cozy together at the sides using mattress stitch (see page 25) and A. Oversew the lower seam from the inside. From the outside, oversew the Flap in place along the top of the back.

Sew the button in place using a separated strand of B.

Pencil pot

Skills needed:
- **Cast on**
- **Bind (cast) off**
- **Knit**
- **Purl**
- **Follow pattern repeats**
- **Join in a new color**
- **Joining seams**

If you're tired of seeing pens and pencils lying around, now is the time to knit them their very own home. This simple pot, worked in an easy alternating knit/purl pattern known as seed (moss) stitch, is an ideal second project for new knitters. Once you've mastered the basics, you'll easily be able to work out how to knit these containers in different sizes to suit all your storage needs!

YARN
Sirdar Click Chunky with Wool (70% acrylic, 30% wool) bulky (chunky) yarn:
  1 x 1¾oz/50g ball (82yd/75m) in shade 146 Bloom (A)
Rowan Pure Wool DK (100% wool) light worsted (DK) yarn:
  Small amount in shade 030 Damson (B)

NEEDLES AND EQUIPMENT
Size US size 6 (4mm) knitting needles
Yarn sewing needle

GAUGE (TENSION)
18 sts and 32 rows in pattern to a 4-in (10-cm) square using A on US size 6 (4mm) needles.

MEASUREMENTS
The pencil pot is 4¼in (11cm) tall.

ABBREVIATIONS
k = knit
p = purl
rep = repeat
st(s) = stitch(es)
WS = wrong side
[ ] = denotes a sequence of stitches to be repeated the number of times given after the brackets

For the pot
Sides
(make 1)
Cast on 54 sts in A.
Row 1: [K1, p1] to end.
Row 2: [P1, k1] to end.
Rep these 2 rows 16 times more.

Break yarn and join in B, using yarn double—see Note on page 89 under Gauge (Tension).
Next row: K.
Bind (cast) off.

Base
(make 1)
Cast on 14 sts in A.
Row 1: [K1, p1] to end.
Row 2: [P1, k1] to end.
Rep last 2 rows 11 times more.
Bind (cast) off.

Making up and finishing
Weave in all loose ends.

Turn Sides piece so it is WS outward. Using A, join the short edges together using mattress stitch (see page 25).

Place the Base in position on the bottom of the Sides so that the back seam of the Sides is in the center of the bound-(cast-) off edge of the Base. Oversew right around all the edges of the Base from the inside to secure it to the Sides.

Suppliers

USA

KNITTING FEVER INC.
www.knittingfever.com
Debbie Bliss, Katia, Sirdar, Sublime

LION BRAND YARNS
Tel: +800 258 YARN (9276)
Online sales and store locator on website
www.lionbrand.com

WESTMINSTER FIBERS
Tel: +800 445 9276
www.westminsterfibers.com
Rowan

CANADA

DIAMOND YARN
www.diamondyarn.com
Debbie Bliss, Katia, Sirdar, Sublime

PATONS
Tel: +1 888 368 8401
www.yarninspirations.com

WESTMINSTER FIBERS
Tel: +800 263 2354
www.westminsterfibers.com
Rowan

UK

Retailers:
DERAMORES
Online store only
www.deramores.com

LAUGHING HENS
Online store only
Tel: +44 (0) 1829 740903
www.laughinghens.com
Cascade, Debbie Bliss, Patons, Rowan, Sublime

JOHN LEWIS
Retail stores and online
www.johnlewis.com
Telephone numbers of local stores on website
Debbie Bliss, Patons, Rowan, Sirdar

LOVEKNITTING.COM
Online store only
www.loveknitting.com
Cascade, Debbie Bliss, Katia, Lion Brand, Patons, Rowan, Sirdar, Sublime

MAVIS CRAFTS
Online and retail store
44 High Street
Bushey
WD23 3HL
Tel: +44 (0) 208 950 5445
www.mavis-crafts.com
Katia, Sirdar, Sublime

Brands:
DEBBIE BLISS YARNS
www.debbieblissonline.com
Tel: +44 (0) 1535 664222

KATIA YARNS
Tel: +34 93 828 38 19
www.katia.com
Website gives details of local suppliers in the UK.

PATONS
Tel: +44 (0) 1484 681881
www.makeitcoats.co.uk

ROWAN YARNS
Tel: +44 (0) 1484 681881
www.knitrowan.com

SIRDAR
Tel: +44 (0) 1924 231682
www.sirdar.co.uk

AUSTRALIA

BLACK SHEEP WOOL 'N' WARES
www.blacksheepwool.com.au
Debbie Bliss, Katia, Patons, Sirdar, Sublim

PRESTIGE YARNS PTY LTD
Tel: +61 (0) 2 4285 6669
www.prestigeyarns.com.au
Debbie Bliss

ROWAN
www.knitrowan.com
Online store locator

SUN SPUN
185 Canterbury Road
Canterbury
Victoria
VIC 3126
Tel: +61 (0) 3 9830 1609
www.sunspun.com.au
Debbie Bliss, Rowan, Sublime

TEXYARNS INTERNATIONAL PTY LT
Tel: +61 (0) 3 9427 9009
www.texyarns.com
Katia

YARN OVER
Shop 1, 265 Blaker Road
Keperra
QLD 4054
Tel: +61 (0) 7 3851 2608
Patons

Index

Acknowledgments

My thanks to Cindy Richards, Penny Craig, Fahema Khanam, and everyone at CICO Books for their ideas and support. Thanks also to Kate Haxell and Marie Clayton, my editors, and Marilyn Wilson, the pattern checker; to photographers Terry Benson and Caroline Arber, and stylists Luis Peral, Sophie Martell, and Nel Haynes. I would also like to thank my ever-patient husband Roger Dromard and our son Louis, my sister Louise Turner for her help with the knitting, and Rowan Yarns for supplying much of the yarn used in these patterns.